Rural Banking and Poverty Alleviation

RURAL BANKING AND POVERTY ALLEVIATION

(A Case Study of West Bengal)

Bhaktapada Sinha Roy

ABHIJEET PUBLICATIONS

DELHI 110 094

ABHIJEET PUBLICATIONS
2/46 Tukhmeerpur Extension
Delhi 110 094
Phone: 22960492, 65698474
e-mail: abhijeet_singh@vsnl.net
abhijeet_singh@indiatimes.com
abhijeetpublication@gmail.com

RURAL BANKING AND POVERTY ALLEVIATION

First Published 2007

ISBN 81-89886-13-4
(Price: Rs. 450/- INR)

PRINTED IN INDIA

Published by J.K. Singh for Abhijeet Publications, Delhi 110094, Lasertypeset by Rajesh Data Services, New Delhi and Printed at Himanshu Printers, Delhi.

To

Chhabi, Rana & Ria

Preface

Important developments took place in the Indian Banking system during the last three decades foremost of which is the establishment of Regional Rural Banks. The Regional Rural Banks epitomise a serious enterprise toward bringing the remotest parts of the rural area within the fold of an organised system. In the absence of such an organisationl network national planning for economic development of the country could not hope to achieve sizeable success. The present work entitled 'Rural Banking and Poverty Alleviation' is devoted to the study of the Regional Rural Banks of the West Bengal.

Apart from using various official records and reports, the author of this study took trips to the Chairmen of the Regional Rural Banks of West Bengal and Managers of some of their branches for the collection of relevant data which are incorporated in the present volume.

The work was done during the period 1980-1984 under the guidance and supervision of Professor G.C. Mandal for which I am grateful to him.

My sincere thanks are also due to all the chairmen of the Regional Rural Banks and their Branch Managers for their assistance and whole-hearted cooperation in conducting the case studies.

I am highly indebted to my Professor Late Dr. G.C. Mandal who taught me how to write scholarly books.

My wife Chhabi and sister-in-law Dali inspired me very much for publiscation of this book.

My former student Mr. Subrata Kumar Nayek, Proprietor of Books and Periodicals, Bolpur, West Bengal helped me much for finding out a suitable publisher for the book. The young and energetic publisher Mr. Abhijeet Singh readily agreed to publish the book for which I am grateful to him. My sincere thanks are due to Subrata and Abhijeet.

I also appreciate very much the help of my son Surajit Sinha Roy, M.A. in checking the manuscripts. I of course, retain the full responsibility for any errors which remain.

BHAKTAPADA SINHA ROY

Contents

Contents

Abbreviations Used

BGB	Bardhaman Gramin Bank
CRAFICARD	Committee to Review Arrangements for Institutional Credit for Agriculture and Rural Development
DIC	District Industrial Centre
DCC	District Coordination Committee
DRDA	District Rural Development Authority
DRI	Differential Rate of Interest
DICGC	Deposit Insurance and Credit Guarantee Corporation
DCP	District Credit Plan
DCCB	District Central Cooperative Bank
FSS	Farmers Service Societies
GIC	General Insurance Corporation
GGB	Gaur Gramin Bank
IRD	Institute of Rural Development

IRDP	Integrated Rural Development Programme
IDBI	Industrial Development Bank of India
LDB	Land Development Bank
MGB	Mayurakshi Gramin Bank
MBGB	Mallabhum Gramin Bank
NGB	Nadia Gramin Bank
NIBM	National Institute of Bank Management
PACS	Primary Agricultural Credit Societies
RBI	Reserve Bank of India
RRB	Regional Rural Bank
SGB	Sagar Gramin Bank
UBKGB	Uttar Banga Kshetriya Gramin Bank

PART I

1

Introduction

The rise of Regional Rural Banks constitutes a landmark in the development of the Indian Banking System.

Traditionally the rural sector of the Indian economy had always been handicapped by dearth of finance capital. While, in the wake of frequent crop-failures due to natural calamities and great trade-depression, the burden of rural indebtedness had been mounting day by day the grip of private money-lenders over the Indian cultivators was being tightened everywhere in the country. Thus, the impoverishment of the peasantry was growing fast and the stagnation of agriculture was perpetuated, leaving no way out of the rut.

Emergence of the cooperative movement mostly centered on the establishment of cooperative credit societies and cooperative banks was a step in the right direction. However, for various reasons mainly lack of vigorous leadership and production-oriented policy the cooperatives failed to make deep dent into the problem of rural credit and emancipate the peasantry from the clutches of the private money lenders. The weaknesses and shortcomings of the cooperative movement were too deep rooted to be overcome easily as a consequence of which it virtually fell into a moribund condition.

The expansion of the commercial banking system particularly following the nationalization of 14 banks in 1969 and efforts to revive the cooperative movement by State Participation touched only the peripheries of the rural economy, most of it being left to the mercy of private agencies.

The realization of the need of a specialised institution like Rural Banks to be specially concerned with the weaker sections of the rural community was becoming more and more pronounced until it was actually incorporated in the Report of the Banking Commission in 1972. The actual establishment of 5 Regional Rural Banks in 1975 followed the recommendations of the working group on Rural Banks under the Chairmanship of M. Narasimham (Chapter 3).

The objective of the present study is to trace the evolution of rural banking and probe the structural and operational models of rural banks in India and, against this context, to critically evaluate the structure and functioning of the Regional Rural Banks of West Bengal on the basis of case studies. The scope of the work is restricted to a specialized study of the RRBs of West Bengal though it also covers the study of rural credit provided by cooperative banks and also glimpses of the role of commercial banks in rural areas. This is because, as will be elaborated later, the RRBs are wholly concerned with credit for rural areas to meet credit needs of the weaker sections of the rural community.

This volume consists of two parts. In addition to the introductory chapter Part I comprises 2 more chapters. Chapter 2 is devoted to the analysis and discussion of the rural economy of West Bengal which will enable one to estimate the importance of rural credit specifically in this state. Chapter 3 traces the genesis of rural banking, its aims and objectives, evolution, structural and operational models, its finance and various problems of management on the basis of various official reports and other relevant literature already available. This chapter may be considered as the theoretical background, thrashing out the principles involved in the light of which the assessment of actual practice is made possible.

Part II comprises Chapter 4 dealing with the present status of rural credit in West Bengal from the point of view of its demand and supply. Chapter 5 devoted to case studies of 7 Regional Rural Banks in the context of the characteristics of their area of operation. Chapter 6 related to the discussion of rates of interest on deposits, borrowings and lendings and mode of loaning operations of RRBs, Chapter 7 attempting a comparative assessment of the performance of the Regional Rural Banks of West Bengal, Chapter 8 containing some reflections on structural and operational problems of the Regional Rural Banks and Chapter 9 presenting the summary and conclusions of the entire study.

In conducting the case studies the present research worker had to face a number of difficulties foremost of which is the lack of uniform standard of keeping records by the different Regional Rural Banks and their branches. The matter has been discussed in Appendix to Chapter 7. Thus the task of making a comparative assessment by reducing the Regional Rural Banks to a common denominator was made difficult. However, the task was attempted by a proper sifting of facts and careful interpretation.

The case studies of the Regional Rural Banks were conducted during the period 1980-82 and, therefore, could cover only those Regional Rural Banks which were started before 1982. These were seven in number, namely, Gaur Gramin Bank, Mayurakshi Gramin Bank, Mallabhum Gramin Bank, Uttarbanga Kshetriya Gramin Bank, Sagar Gramin Bank, Bardhaman Gramin Bank and Nadia Gramin Bank. Howrah Gramin Bank being started in June, 1982 could not provide any data for its evaluation.

The case studies based upon material drawn from interviews with the Chairmen and branch managers of the seven Regional Rural Banks, involving a travel for the purpose attempts to indicate how far these banks were able to serve as an agency for the mobilization of rural savings and for channelling credit to concerns or people where it was most needed. Further, the case studies were directed towards assessing the growth potential of the Regional Rural Banks and their operational efficiency.

In spite of difficulties the study had to face, it can claim to be an attempt to gather knowledge about a field hitherto unexplored.

2

Rural Economy of West Bengal: Structure and Problems

Population, Climate, Topography and Soil

West Bengal is one of the Eastern States of Indian Union with an area of 87,853 sq. km. and with a population of 5,44,85,560.

In the Himalayan Division the weather of West Bengal is delightfully cool during summer. In winter in some areas of Darjeeling the temperature goes below the freezing point. Most of the rains in this region come between May and October. The rainfall in the remaining months is negligible. In the plains the cool weather starts by about the middle of November and lasts upto the middle of February. The rainfall is scanty during this period. From the end of February the weather begins to warm up. During March and April there is rapid rise of temperature and the month of May records the highest maximum temperatures. With the coming of the monsoon in June, the temperature begins to fall steadily and the cool season starts in November.

The land area of West Bengal can be divided into four broad agro-climatic regions. The first is an extension of the Chhotanagpur Plateau which comprises the districts of Purulia and the continguous western parts of the districts of Midnapore and Bankura, Burdwan and Birbhum. This region is characterized by laterite soil covering 23,98,000 hectares of cropped area (33.12% of the total cropped area). The second is the mountainous northern zone (hilly-terrain comprising parts of the districts of Darjeeling, Jalpaiguri, West Dinajpur and Coochbehar covering 8,42,000 hectares of cropped area (11.58% of the total). The third covering the districts of Howrah, Hooghly, Burdwan, Nadia, Malda, Murshidabad, northern part of 24 Parganas lies in the Gangetic plains rich in alluvial soils. The cropped area belonging to this region is 28,89,000 hectares (39.87% of the total). The fourth one is the coastal region consisting of southern part of 24 Parganas, Midnapur and Howrah. The cropped area of this region is 11,42,000 hectares (14.31% of the total).

In the hilly-terrain of the north of West Bengal the soil is podsolic which is suitable for growing tea. The soil of the laterite region is composed of sandy clay loam and clay loam with concretion. The soils are deficient in lime and organic matter. The plains of the north and south of the state fall within the Gangetic alluvial tract containing supserior quality of soil highly suitable for cultivation of different varieties of crops. The tracts of Sundarbans and lower Midnapur, however, have a high percentage of salt in the soil which is unsuitable for cultivation.[1]

According to the census of 1981 West Bengal has a population of 5,44,85,560 persons, comprising 2,85,05,151 males and 2,59,80,409 females. According to the census of 1981 rural population of West Bengal is 4,00,52,074 (74% of the total) and urban population is 1,44,33,486 of the total (26% of the total).

The percentage distribution of rural workers of West Bengal vis-a-vis that of all India as between different occupations is presented in Table 2.1.

Table 2.1

The Occupational Structure of the Rural Work Force

Category of Workers	*West Bengal (per cent)*	*All India (per cent)*
Cultivators	43.07	51.61
Agricultural Labourers	34.99	30.69
Livestock, Forestry, Fishing, Hunting, Plantations, Orchard and Allied Activities	3.73	2.53
Agricultural Sector Workforce	81.79	84.83
Mining and Quarrying	1.20	0.41
Household Industry	2.64	3.21
Other than Household Industry	3.66	2.29
Construction	0.54	0.74
Trade and Commerce	3.01	2.44
Transport, Storage and Communication	1.37	0.82
Other Services	5.79	5.26
Total Non-Agricultural Workers	18.21	15.17
Total Workforce	100.00	100.00

Source: Census of India, 1971.

1a. Agro-Economic Research Centre, Visva-Bharati, Agricultural Development in West Bengal - Mimeograph 1977, Vol. I & II.

1b. D.K. Dasgupta, "Regional Inbalamcences in Agricultural Growth in West Bengal, Need for Appraisal and a New Strategy", in *Rural Development—Action and Management*, edited by Madhu S. Mishra, Indian Institute of Management, Calcutta-1981.

It is evident from Table 2.1 that the occupational pattern of rural West Bengal is more or less the same as that of India as a whole. The rural economy of West Bengal is predominantly agricultural keeping about 82 per cent of its workers engaged in agriculture, about 6 per cent in industry, 3 per cent in trade and commerce and the rest in other occupations.

Cropping Pattern

Gross cropped area in West Bengal was 71,52,000 hectares in 1970-71. Ratio of irrigated area to cultivated area was 29.87% in 1970-71.[2]

Foodgrains occupied the predominant position in the cropping pattern of the state. Among the foodgrains, rice is the single most important crop grown in West Bengal. It formed more than the 70 per cent of the cropped area in 1971-72. Rice is grown in three seasons, viz. autumn, winter and summer; of them winter rice constituted more than 75 per cent of the total rice. Summer rice (locally known as boro) which accounted for only 0.3% of the area in 1950-51 claimed as much as 4.49% of the cropped area in 1973-74. With the introduction of HYV rice and improved irrigation facilities in the summer season, the boro paddy had come to occupy a very significant place in some districts of West Bengal. Similar was the case with wheat which made tremendous progress in respect of the area with the introduction of exotic varieties of wheat. The percentage of area under other crops remained practically

2. *Source:* Govt. of West Bengal Bureau of Applied Economics and Statistics, Statistical Handbook, 1979, p. 1. Also, Agro-Economic Research Centre, Visva Bharati, Agricultural Development of West Bengal, 1951-52, to 1973-74.

unchanged. The cropping pattern that was prevalent in West Bengal in 1978-79 is presented in Table 2.2.

Table 2.2 shows that predominance of foodgrains in the crop-economy of West Bengal continued in 1978-79, covering 85 per cent of the total cropped area. Coverage of rice declined from 70.59 per cent of 1971-72 to 68 per cent of the total cropped area in 1978-79 owing to emergence of other crops like wheat, oilseeds, potato etc. Extension of high yielding boro rice and wheat marked the year. Oil seeds which cover 3.44 per cent of the cropped area assumed importance because of their high profitability. Potato, too, occupying 2.30 per cent of the cropped area has assumed pride of place in the agricultural economy of West Bengal.

Land Use Pattern

It can be seen from Table 2.3 that out of the total land area (8,849,000 hectares) of West Bengal, 56,47,000 hectares (63.8 per cent of the total) are covered by net sown area. Forests (reserved) cover 11,86,000 hectares, constituting 13.4 per cent of the total area. Forests are a valuable resource and as they are mostly located in the neighbourhood of villages, they have great importance in the rural economy of West Bengal. Current fallows to the extent of 70,000 hectares, constituting 0.8 per cent and other uncultivated lands (6,20,000 hectares) constituting 7.0 per cent of the total area await profitable utilization.

Table 2.2
Area Under Principal Crops (1978-79)

S.No.	*Foodgrains*	*Thousand Hectares (1978-79)*	*Total (per cent)*
1.	**Cereals**		
	Rice	4765	67.93
	Aus	695	9.90
	Aman	3628	51.73
	Boro	442	6.30
	Wheat	521	7.42
	Barley	35	
	Maize	47	
	Other cereals	28	
	Total cereals	5396	76.93
	Pulses		
	Gram	100	
	Arhar	13	
	Other kharif pulses	32	
	Other rabi pulses	416	
	Total pulses	562	8.00
	Total foodgrains	5957	85.32
2.	**Oil seeds**		
	Rape and mustard	110	
	Linseed	68	
	Other oil seeds	63†	
	Total oil seeds	241†	3.44
3.	**Oil seeds**	32	
4.	**Fibres**		
	Jute	538	
	Mesta	45	
	Cotton	#	
	Other fibres	2	
	Total fibres	585	8.37
5.	**Miscellaneous crops**		
	Potato	161	2.30
	Ginger	2	
	Dry chillies	23	

Tobacco	13	
Tea	*	
Total miscellaneous crops	199	2.84
Grand Total	7014	100.00

† Provisional

Less than 500 hectares

* Not available

Source: Government of West Bengal, Statistical Handbook, 1979.

Table 2.3

Utilization of Land in West Bengal 1977-78

(Area in Thousand Hectares)

Classification	*1977-78*	
	Area	*Percentage*
1. Net area shown	5647	63.8
2. Current fallows	70	0.8
3. Forests (reserved)	1186	13.4
4. Area not available for cultivation	1326	15.0
5. Other uncultivated lands excluding current fallows	620	7.0
Total	8849	100.0

Source: Economic Review 1980-81, Govt. of West Bengal, Calcutta, 1981, p. 58.

Land System

The land system of West Bengal was for a long time governed by the provisions of the permanent settlement which was introduced in 1793 in Bengal as well as in Bihar and Orissa. According to this settlement the landlords would have to pay the Government ten-eleventh of the revenue collected from the tenants. They would enjoy the remaining one-eleventh as their remuneration. But it is found that the landlord started gradually to collect more revenue from the tenants than due to them; but revenue imposed on them by the Government did not increase at all. As a result gradually a vested interest class namely 'Zamindars' emerged in Bengal.

The economic or social objectives for which Lord Cornwallis introduced Permanent Settlement were not fulfilled. First, there is no doubt that collection of revenue was made definite and was well-controlled but there was no increase of due land revenue in case of the Government. On the other hand the ordinary tenants were gradually overburdened with the imposition of rent. Secondly Lord Cornwallis expected the landlords will take part in social development acquiring normal leadership of the society. But the landlords only collected revenue and led luxurious life staying in the town. They did not try to develop land. As a result of this the conditions of agriculture and tenants deteriorated seriously. Again as a result of the permanent settlement different types of intermediary interests arose in addition to the landlords. Before the abolition of Zamindari system there were many intermediaries between the actual tenant farmers and the landlord.

The serious evils of the zamindari system led to legislations for its abolition after independence in the affected states. As a result of these legislations the proprietory rights of the zamindars were acquired by the state on payment of compensation and the statutory tenant or the tenant-in-chief was brought into direct relationship with the state. By the end of March, 1968, the abolition of intermediaries was fully implemented in M.P., Punjab, Assam, Gujarat, Madras, Maharashtra, Rajasthan, Andhra Pradesh, U.P., West Bengal and Kerala.

We give below the highlights of zamindari abolition legislation enacted in different states and for illustrative purpose show the relevant provisions included under the West Bengal Estates Acquisition Act of 1955:—

(*a*) The intermediary rights are abolished and compensation paid to the zamindar.

(*b*) The compensation is paid partly in cash and partly in bonds.

(*c*) The zamindar is allowed to retain land for personal cultivation but, in most cases, a ceiling on land holding is introduced.

(*d*) After the abolition of zamindari system, the tenant is responsible for payment of rent directly to the government.

1. The ceiling area shall be:—

(*a*) In the case of a raiyat, who is an adult unmarried person, 2.50 standard hectares;

(*b*) In the case of a raiyat, who is the sole surviving member of a family, 2.50 standard hectares;

(*c*) In the case of a raiyat having a family consisting of two or more, but not more than five members, 5.00 standard hectares;

(*d*) In the case of a raiyat having a family consisting of more than five members, 5.00 standard hectares plus 0.50 standard hectare for each member in excess of five, so, however, that the aggregate of the ceiling area for such raiyat shall not in any case, exceed 7.00 standard hectares;

(*e*) In the case of any other raiyat, 7.00 standard hectares.

2. Notwithstanding anything contained in (1), where in the family of a raiyat, there are more raiyats than

one, the ceiling area for the raiyat, together with the ceiling area of all the other raiyats in the family shall not, in any case, exceed:—

(*a*) Where the number of members of such family does not exceed five, 5.00 standard hectares;

(*b*) Where such number exceeds five, 5.00 standard hectares, plus 0.50 standard hectare for each member in excess of five, so, however, that the aggregate of the ceiling area shall not, in any case, exceed 7.00 standard hectares.

3. For the purpose of sub-section (2), all the lands owned individually by the members of a family or jointly by some or all the members of such family shall be deemed to be owned by the raiyats in the family.

4. In determining the extent of land owned by the raiyats in a family or the sole surviving member of a family or an adult unmarried person, the share of such raiyat or raiyats, or such sole surviving member, or such adult unmarried person, as the case may be, in the lands owned by a cooperative society, company, cooperative farming society, Hindu undivided family or a firm shall be taken into account.

Table 2.4

Land Distribution Upto June, 1979

(Areas in acres)	
Total agricultural lands vested	11,17,135.94
Area of vested land hit by injunction	1,70,010.05
Area of vested land available for distribution	9,47,125.89
Area of vested land distributed	6,15,503.87
Area of land yet to be distributed	3,31,622.02
Beneficiaries	
Total number of beneficiaries	9,75,032
of which	

Scheduled Castes	3,57,168
Scheduled Tribes	1,92,132

Source: Government of West Bengal, Land Reforms in West Bengal, 1979.

5. The lands owned by a trust on endowment other than of a public nature, shall be deemed to be lands owned by the beneficiaries under the trust or endowment and each such beneficiary shall be deemed to be a raiyat under this act to the extent of the share of his beneficial interest in the said trust or endowment.[3]

Left Front Government's Land Reforms Policy is aimed at improving the economic position of about 63 lakh families directly dependent upon agriculture. An account of the land distribution programme carried out in pursuit of this objective is shown in Table 2.4.

The table above indicates marked progress in regard to distribution of vested land. The table also shows that the main beneficiaries are the members of scheduled castes and scheduled tribes overwhelming majority of whom are landless agricultural labourers and poor peasants.

The Left Front Government has decided to accelerate the tempo of land distribution. Henceforth the Panchayats will be the main vehicle of land distribution. This new decision will go a long way in the distribution of vested lands among the really needy persons.

Operation Barga[4]

Operation Barga is the most important feature of the land reforms policy implemented by the Left Front

3. The West Bengal Land Reforms Act, 1955, West Bengal Act X of 1956.

4(a). Govt. of West Bengal—An Evaluation of a Pledge, 1980.

(b). Govt. of West Bengal—Left Front Govt. and some aspects of its activities in rural areas, 1980.

Government of West Bengal. In recording the names of Bargadars a new style of operation was introduced in September 1978 under the name of "Operation Barga". "Operation Barga" is the most important factor in Left Front Government's total package programme for rural transformation. The operation encouraged share-croppers to register themselves so that the legal rights to the land they cultivate year in and year out could be firmly established.

It is implemented in practice by: *(i)* selecting places where there are concentration of share-croppers, *(ii)* by convening meeting of both the owner and the share-croppers by giving notice to both in all possible legal manner and by beat of drums, *(iii)* to hear both parties and to examine document, if any, *(iv)* to pass judgement, and *(v)* to issue certificates to share-croppers where names have been recorded.

The progress of recent land reforms at a glance is shown in the Table 2.5.

Table 2.5

The Progress of Land Reform in Recent Years

Category	*Number*
1. Recording the names of share-croppers (upto April 30, 1980)	8,54,740
2. House sites legalised to agricultural labourers, poor peasants, poor fishermen, poor artisans etc. (upto 31st December, 1979)	41,077
3. Number of beneficiaries who have received vested land upto 31.3.1980	10,44,425
4. Number of families relieved of land rent for ever	45 Lakhs
5. Bank loans advanced to share-croppers and patta-holders of Benami land	59,114 families
6. Mandays generated upto the end of 1979	5.66 crore i.e. 16.98

crore kgs. of wheat 11.32 crores of rupees the village poor including the agricultural labourers and poor peasants have been able to earn more.

The land ceiling that followed the abolition of the estate system during the 1950s and the doling out of surplus lands to marginal or sub-marginal tillers and landless labourers might have exerted an influence on the distribution of operational holding shown in Table 2.6.

Table 2.6

Distribution of Operational Holdings in West Bengal

Size-class	*Percentage of No. of Holdings*		*Percentage of Area*	
	1970-71	*1976-77*	*1970-71*	*1976-77*
Below 1.0	59.97	66.48	21.53.	27.15
1.0 - 2.0	22.33	20.55	25.75	28.54
2.0 - 4.0	13.23	10.38	28.94	27.09
4.0 - 10.0	4.38	2.55	19.23	13.25
10.0 & above	0.09	0.04	4.58	3.97
Total	100.00	100.00	100.00	100.00

Source: Agricultural Census 1976-77, Board of Revenue, Directorate of Agriculture, Government of West Bengal, 1979, p. 10.

Table 2.6 indicates that both the percentage of number of holdings and area for farm-size classes above 4 hectares declined. Thus, during 1970-71 farms above 4 hectares constituting 4.47 per cent of total had under them 24 per cent of the land area. By 1976-77 their number declined to 2.59 per cent commanding 17 per cent of the total land area. Even in the size-class 2-4 hectares there was a decline both in the proportion of holdings and area under them. But remarkably enough number of holdings below 1.0 hectare increased from 60 per cent to 66 per cent with area increasing from 22 per cent to 27 per cent.

The average size of operational holding in West Bengal declined from 1.20 hectares of 1970-71 to 0.99 hectares of 1976-77.[5]

As a consequence of the fact that the surplus land vested in the Government are being distributed among sub-marginal farmers and landless labourers, increasing the number of tiny farmers, the problem of viability of farms arising from their insignificant size is immensely magnified.

By the standard of minimum caloric requirement the rural poverty of West Bengal is greater than that of many other states. Thus, while the average percentage of population in rural India consuming less than minimum calorie needs (FAO minimum 2750 K calories per consumer unit) is 54, in West Bengal 73 per cent of the rural population are below this minimum-calorie-intake-standard.[6]

According to the All India Debt and Investment Survey 1971-72 by the Reserve Bank of India while the all-India average asset of a cultivator and an agricultural labourer amounted to Rs. 14,694.00 and Rs. 1139.00 respectively, the average asset for a West Bengal cultivator

5. Source: Ibid.
6. S. Sengupta and P.D. Joshi, "A note on the determination of poverty line based on National Sample Survey 27th Round Data", *Sarvekshan*, Vol. III, No. 1, July, 1979.

and agricultural labourer worked out to Rs. 9965.00 and Rs. 578.00 respectively.

Thus the role of Rural Banks in the removal of rural poverty is greater in West Bengal than many other states. The Rural Banks being specifically committed to meeting the credit requirements of the weaker sections of the community will have to face a stupendous problem precipitated by the independent status acquired by a large number of tiny tillers and Bargadars who might have been tied so long to the patron-client relationship with their masters.

Increased credit requirements due to the advent of the High Yielding Variety technology and extension of summer rice, oilseed and potato area is another factor that adds to the financial responsibility of the Rural Banks for poor cultivators. In West Bengal this responsibility is much greater than in other parts of the country in view of all the facts of its rural economy stated above.

Village Industries: Problems of Development

Among the village and small-scale industries in West Bengal mention may be made of the following industries:

1. Brass metal and bell metal industry
2. Handloom industry
3. Small scale units producing machine parts and engineering goods
4. Sericulture
5. Bamboo work
6. Wood work

7. Leather industry
8. Village pottery
9. Blacksmithy
10. Net making (for piciculture)
11. Bidi binding
12. Minor employment sectors (Goldsmithy, conch shell making, cutting and tailoring, embroidery etc.)

The problems of the above-mentioned village and small scale industries are more or less common and can be summarised as follows:

1. Lack of adequate capital is one of the major problems on the part of the poor artisans of the village and small scale industries.
2. The artisans suffer very much as there is no regular and adequate source of supply of raw materials for their product.
3. Outdated method and technique of production of these industries is another problem which stands in the way of their expansion and development.
4. These industries face competition both from the products of the large-scale industries and imported goods.
5. Marketing difficulty is the most important problem of these industries. The artisans do not get fair price for their product due to exploitation of so many middlemen and inferior quality of their product.
6. The large scale units making purchases from the smaller units often do not pay the dues of the latter.
7. Another problem is concerned with the reluctance

on the part of big industries in the state to place orders with them.

Table 2.7 presents data on the distribution of employment in small scale industrial units among different districts of the state. It appears from the table that most of the small scale industrial units are located in Calcutta, 24-Parganas and Howrah because of the availability of infrastructural facilities in these districts under the impact of urban development.

Table 2.7

Number of Small Scale Industrial Units Registered with the Cottage and Small Scale Industries with Corresponding Employment in the District of West Bengal

Upto 1979-80 (31.3.80)

	District	*Unit**	*Employment**
1.	Burdwan	9340	57309
2.	Birbhum	4350	34692
3.	Bankura	5120	32817
4.	Midnapur	7597	58002
5.	Howrah	15924	190472
6.	Hooghly	6471	55399
7.	24-Parganas	17691	164933
8.	Calcutta	29085	282460
9.	Nadia	6659	59521
10.	Murshidabad	8625	51474
11.	West Dinajpur	2511	10467
12.	Malda	2712	14593
13.	Jalpaiguri	2665	16735
14.	Darjeeling	3434	24476
15.	Cooch Behar	2490	16700
16.	Purulia	3870	25400
	Total	1,28,553	10,95,451

* Estimated

Source: Directorate of Cottage and Small Scale Industries, West Bengal.

The Regional Rural Banks should have thorough awareness of the nature, extent and the problems of the small-scale industrial units as well as the village industries. Their development would reduce dependence on agriculture, create new employment opportunities and enhance incomes of the rural workers engaged in this sector. As such, the Rural Banks are expected to play a crucial role in accelerating this process.

3

Genesis of Rural Banking

The policy in respect of rural credit since 1951 was to widen the role of the institutional credit agencies toward replacement of the non-institutional credit agencies, specially the private money-lenders as far as possible.

Finding of the All India Rural Credit Survey Report of 1951-52 revealed that cooperative credit institutions played an almost insignificant role in extending credit to the agriculturists. In 1951-52, only 3.1 per cent of the total credit needs of the cultivators were met by them. Governmental agencies supplied an equal proportion and the rest of the credit needs were met by professional and agriculturist money lenders. Other concerned committees, too, pointed out similar problems in dealing with this question. The rate of interest charged by the money-lenders was exorbitant—much above the maximum rate prescribed by the state governments and very often it was out of proportion to the risk involved.

They were able to resort to questionable practices because of the "helplessness, ignorance and the necessity of the borrowers".[1] These practices included: *(a)* demand for advance rent, *(b)* demand for a present for doing business known as girah kholai (purse opening), *(c)* taking of thumb impression on a blank paper with a view to inserting any arbitrary amount at a later date if the debtor becomes irregular in payment of interest, *(d)* general manipulation of the accounts to the disadvantage of the debtor, *(e)* insertion of written documents of sums considerably in excess of the actual money lent, and *(f)* taking of conditional sale deeds in order to provide against possible evasion of payment by the debtor.[2]

To these may be added, possible exploitation of the poor borrowers through their contractual obligation to sell output only through the money-lender at a price lower than what could have been obtained in the market.[3] The poor villagers are permanently tied to the money-lender by perpetual poverty in which their expenses exceed their income every year compelling them to take loans.

On an examination of the strengths and weaknesses of the rural credit system dominated by the non-institutional credit agencies, the All India Rural Credit Survey Committee recommended the organisation of multipurpose cooperatives which will provide integrated credit facilities linking production with marketing of inputs and outputs, processing and warehousing activities offered only viable remedy to the credit problems of the villages of India.[4]

On the basis of recommendation of the All India Rural Credit Survey Committee the Government of India lent its support to creating a three-tier cooperative credit structure consisting of an apex body at the state level

(State Cooperative Bank), an intermediary layer of District Central Cooperative Bank (DCCB or simply CCB)—at the district level and the 'primary' credit societies at the base level. The primary credit societies were divided into primary agricultural credit societies (PACS) and primary non-agricultural credit societies. The latter were meant for meeting the needs of rural credit for non-agricultural purposes. PACS could further be classified into 'small-sized agricultural credit societies' and 'large-sized agricultural credit societies'.

In the cooperative structure of rural credit, a distinction was made between two types of cooperatives which would lend short and medium-term loans and Land Development Banks (LDBs) which would provide only medium and long-term loans for the development of agriculture.

The national commission on ag iculture had strongly urged the formation of 'Farmers Service Societies' (FSS) at the base level as a new cooperative society or formed out of a group of societies which would provide an integrated package of service to the farmers including the supply of inputs and facilities for marketing of the produce. Thus a number of FSS appeared on the rural credit scene.

The commercial bank in India had been lending a negligible part of their funds to the rural areas. In view of the large gap between credit needs of modern agriculture and the supply of credit for this sector the government accepted the idea of a multi-agency approach to the development of credit institutions which was recommended by the All India Rural Credit Review Committee, 1969. Bank nationalisation which enormously widened the role of commercial banks by urging them to open branches in the rural area more and more was in tune with this policy. Further pursuance of the above policy was evident in the establishment of linkage between cooperatives at the grassroot level and the commercial banks and involvement of the latter in the organisation of farmer service societies, village adoption schemes for the concentration of investment enterprise in compact areas was a part of the process of rural orientation of the commercial banks.

Prior to the coming of the Regional Rural Banks in 1975 the following institutional agencies were engaged in the provision of various types of rural credit[5]; primary Agricultural Credit Societies, concerned government departments, scheduled commercial banks extending direct finance to rural borrowers for short-term and medium-term, primary agricultural credit societies, land development banks and scheduled commercial banks making medium and long-term loans, state cooperative banks and scheduled commercial banks extending short-term indirect finance to rural borrowers through primary cooperatives, scheduled commercial banks, central land development banks and rural electrification corporation granting medium-term and long-term rural credit and, finally, the Reserve Bank of India playing the role of refinancing agency for rural borrowings.

Agriculture has been recognized by the Reserve Bank of India as the 'priority' sector for credit to which contributions of both cooperative and commercial banks made appreciable progress in the course of time. Thus by 1974 share of credit granted by cooperatives in total rural borrowings increased by more than 25 per cent over that of 1951.[6] By April 1977 rural branches of the scheduled commercial banks commanded 37.7 per cent of their total branches which amounted to an increase of 400 per cent over June 1969. During this period share of agricultural credit dispensed by them increased from 5.37 per cent to 10.44 per cent total credit.[7]

In spite of the tremendous growth of the cooperatives and commercial banks for the supply of rural credit in the country overtime the non-institutional credit still continued to account for two-thirds of the total agricultural credit in the country. Still there were vast areas beyond the reach of the banking system.[8] Moreover, the input-intensive modern technology greatly increased the credit requirements of agriculture, particularly because adequate credit could enable even the millions of small and marginal farmers to obtain access to the benefits of the modern agricultural technology in terms of higher productivity. It was difficult for the cooperative and commercial banks to cope with the vast demand of both working and fixed capital arising from agriculture in transition to the modern technology.[9]

In this context the capacity of the existing institutions in the field of rural credit came under review and it was felt that a new type of institution like Regional Rural Banks would be necessary to strengthen their efforts.

The major weaknesses of the cooperatives, specially at the level of the Primary Agricultural Credit Societies (PACS) may be summarised as follows:

1. Uneven distribution of success, substantial success in some areas being accompanied by limited success in other areas.
2. Dormancy conditions and non-viability of many primary village cooperative societies members of which availing themselves of loan facilities are only 38 per cent of the total members.
3. Poor access of small cultivators and weaker sections of the rural community to cooperative credit.

4. Poor administrative condition.

It is acknowledged that most of the institutional rural credit was captured by landlords and rich farmers for lending to poor cultivators, tenants and landless agricultural labourers at higher rates.

Data furnished by All India Debt and Investment Survey 1971-72 indicate that poor assets-groups (upto Rs. 1000/-) could fetch only 6 per cent of their total debt from institutional agencies compared to the corresponding figure of 31 per cent for all cultivators, the corresponding figures for artisans and average rural household being 5 per cent and 29 per cent respectively.

Overdue loans of the PACS went on rising till they stood at 43 per cent of June 1976.[10] "Cases of book adjustment of old loans through renewals which overstate the amount of repayments were not rare".[11]

Equity capital of the PACS appeared to be very meagre (20% of working capital) at the end of June 1976. Their deposits formed only 6 per cent of their working capital at this time. In view of poor owned capital and overdue loans 70 per cent of the primary societies and 52 per cent of the Central Cooperative Banks was recorded as 'weak' in the report of audit inspection.

The farmers service societies which were expected to be instrumental to the working of the cooperatives were marked by their miserable failure both in respect of their magnitude and achievements. As a consequence the very concept of FSS was held in question.

The commercial banks also had their own weaknesses. Substantial growth in the number of rural branches did not result in their deep penetration into the rural areas. Also, their operations did not go beyond mopping up rural deposits for investment in urban areas, triggering a reverse flow of funds from the rural to the urban areas.

Small agricultural borrowers whose borrowings were placed in the category of Rupees Ten Thousand and less could command only 36.53 per cent of the total commercial bank credit at the end of June, 1974.

The linkage between commercial banks and cooperative societies was still inadequately developed, the former financing only 1.79 per cent of primary agricultural credit societies at the end of June, 1976.

High cost structure of commercial banking was a deterrent to its branching out extensively in rural areas. Its social approach was not commensurate with its efficiency.

There was growing need of a type of institution which could combine efficiency with low cost and a democratic approach to meet the vastly increasing credit needs of the small and marginal farmers, rural artisans and the weaker sections of the rural areas.

THE BANKING COMMISSION'S PROPOSAL

Such a type of institution was first visualised by the Banking Commission of 1969 which was convinced of the limitations of the commercial banking practices and doubtful about the potentiality of commercial banks towards satisfaction of the rural needs.

The Banking Commission felt that maximum possible branch expansion of commercial banks might not be able to bridge the gap between supply of and demand for credit in rural areas. Its obvious recommendation was, therefore, in favour of the establishment of a special type of bank, namely, 'rural banks' which could function either as cooperative banks or as subsidiary banks of commercial banks. 51 per cent of the capital of a rural subsidiary bank will be held by the sponsoring bank and the balance by the people in the local areas of its operation. It was further stipulated that the rural banks—whether rural cooperative banks or rural subsidiary banks—would extend credit and all other banking facilities not only to their members (or share-holders) but also to the general public in their own local areas of operation by creating a new class of 'associate members'. The proportion of credit to be given to the members and other conditions for granting such credit may be fixed in advance at more favourable terms than to the associate members. In the view of the Commission, it should be 'possible to organise rural banks for a compact group of villages'.

The Banking Commission drew up the details of structure of a model rural bank in respect of capital, management, personnel, dividend policy, deposit insurance, interest-rate, relationship with government agencies, area of operation etc.

No step, however, was taken to implement the recommendations of the banking commission until after the middle of June, 1975.

The proposal of setting up 'rural banks' came to the fore in the wake of the 'Twenty Point Programme' or 'New Economic Programme' of July 1975, initiated by Mrs. Indira Gandhi, the then Prime Minister, which included drastic measures for liquidating rural indebtedness. Much as they were socially desirable they led to the scaring and drying up of traditional sources of credit for rural people. Such a situation accentuated the need of new alternative sources of credit to meet the requirements of the weaker sections of the rural society. Such alternatives could be provided by 'rural banks' with "attitudinal and operational ethos different from those obtaining in the public sector banks".

In further pursuance of this idea the Government of India appointed a working group on rural banks under the chairmanship of M. Narasimham to 'examine in depth the setting up of new rural banks as subsidiaries of public sector banks to cater to the credit needs of the rural people'. This working group was appointed on 1st July, 1975 and was asked to submit its report within the short period of one month. The report was submitted by the working group on 30th July, 1975.[12] In accordance with the recommendations of the working group on rural banks five regional rural banks were established in the first instance on 2nd October, 1975, their locations being Malda in West Bengal, Jaipur in Rajasthan, Bhiwani in Haryana and Moradabad and Gorakhpur in Uttar Pradesh.

Retrospectively, the RRBs came into existence at a time when, in spite of unequivocal recognition of the need of extending banking facilities into the remotest parts of the rural areas the fulfilment of this need through the cooperative system lagged far behind the intellectual conviction it carried and when it was evident that commercial banks, too, did not play any part more significant than being instrumental to channelling rural savings to urban areas.

REFERENCES

1. Govt. of India, Report of the Agricultural Finance Sub-Committee, New Delhi, 1945, p. 59.
2. Govt. of India, Department of Revenue and Banking, Report

of the Expert Committee on Consumption Credit (Chairman, B. Sivaraman), New Delhi, April 1976, Chap. 6.

4. RBI, All India Rural Credit Survey, Vo.. II, op. cit., chapters VIII, and IX.
5. RBI, Report on Currency and Finance, Vol. I, 1976-77, pp. 131-32.
6. Report of the Expert Committee on Construction Credit, op. cit., Chapter 2.
7. Various issues of the RBI Bulletin.
8. Govt. of India, Report of the Committee (Working Group) on Rural Banks, New Delhi, 1975.
9. Govt. of India, Report of the National Commission on Agriculture, New Delhi, 1976, Part XII, Para 55.7.11.
10. Statistical Statements relating to the cooperative movement in India 1975-76, op. cit.
11. All India Rural Credit Survey, Vol. 11, op. cit., p. 218.
12. Report of the Committee on Rural Banks, New Delhi, 1975.

PART II

4

Rural Credit in West Bengal

As in other states, in West Bengal, too, institutional credit covered a negligible part of the total volume of rural credit. Traditionally, by far the largest source of rural credit has been the private money-lenders. Under the Cooperative Societies Acts of 1904 and 1912 the cooperative movement started in West Bengal as well as in other states and it was mostly concerned with co-operative credit societies.

Prior to the nationalisation of some commercial banks cooperative credit societies were the only institutional source of rural credit in West Bengal as well as in other states. Cooperative societies provided more credit to agriculture. Besides, cooperative credit societies were involved in more food production, improvement of irrigation system, reclamation of agricultural land, prevention of soil erosion and many other allied activities. Cooperative credit societies also helped to increase industrial production by providing credit to cottage and small scale industries for buying raw materials and improved tools of production.

In the period following the nationalisation of 14 banks there was considerable branch expansion of the commercial banks all over India. In West Bengal the number of branch offices increased from 428 of June 1969 to 1942 of March 1982. For the whole of India Rural Centres (places with population upto 10,000) had a share of the extent of 56 per cent of the additional branch offices.[1] Assuming for West Bengal a similar share of rural centres in the expansion, possibly about 862 branches have gone to the rural centres of the state during 1969-82. Bank credit in West Bengal increased from Rs. 526 crores to Rs. 2596 crores during the same period. It is possible that 25 per cent of the addition (Rs. 2070 crores), that is, an amount of about Rs. 518 crores was released as rural credit.

Turning to cooperatives, it may be seen from the Table 4.1 that the number of total credit societies was 13466 in 1960-61. But this number fell to 10240 in 1980-81. But the number of total non-credit societies increased from 5840 in 1960-61 to 10592 in 1980-81. The number of total societies increased from 19306 in 1960-61 to 20832 in 1980-81.

Table 4.2 shows the number of members of the cooperative societies. It is evident from the table that number of members (in thousand) increased steadily both in the case of cooperative credit societies and cooperative non-credit societies. Number of members of total credit societies was 1372 thousand in 1960-61 which rose to 4122 thousand in 1980-81. Number of members of non-credit societies was 484 thousand in 1960-61 which increased to 1617 thousand in 1980-81.

Table 4.1

Cooperative Movement in West Bengal

S. No.	*Types of Societies*	*1960-61*	*1970-71*	*1976-77*	*1977-78*	*1978-79*	*1979-80*	*1980-81*
I.	Number of Societies							
(a)	Credit Societies							
	1. State & Central Banks	30	22	18	18	18	18	18
	2. Land Mortgaged Banks	13	22	25	25	25	25	25
	3. Agriculture	12768	11905	9197	8575	8387	8232	8143
	4. Non-agriculture	655	1077	1649	1809	1903	1957	2054
	Total Credit Societies	13466	13026	10889	10427	10333	10232	10240
(b)	Total Non-credit Societies	5840	6822	9434	9941	10294	10592	10592
	Total Societies	19306	19848	20323	20368	20627	20824	20832(p)

Table 4.2

Cooperative Movement in West Bengal

S. No.	*Types of Societies*	*1960-61*	*1970-71*	*1976-77*	*1977-78*	*1978-79*	*1979-80*	*1980-81*
II.	Number of Members (in thousand)							
(a)	Credit Societies							
	1. State & Central Banks	15	16	15	13	4	7	17
	2. Land Mortgaged Banks	6	34	69	93	121	139	147
	3. Agriculture	661	1120	1958	2073	2305	2371	2379
	4. Non-agriculture	690	1210	1356	1412	1432	1660	1579
	Total Credit Societies	1372	2380	3398	3591	3862	4177	4122
(b)	Total Non-credit Societies	484	776	1015	1052	1277	1617	1617
	Total Societies	1856	3156	4413	4643	5139	5794	5739(p)

Table 4.3 shows the working capital (Rupees in lakhs) of Cooperative Credit Societies in West Bengal. It is evident from the table that working capital increased considerably between 1960-61 to 1980-81 both in the case of cooperative credit societies and cooperative non-credit societies. It may be seen from the table that the working capital of all societies amounted to Rs. 5491 lakhs in 1960-61 which increased to Rupees 74,441 lakhs in 1980-81.

Table 4.4 shows the loans advanced by the Cooperative Credit Societies. It is seen from the table that advances of State and Central Banks, Land Development Banks (Land Mortgage Banks), Cooperative Agricultural Societies and Cooperative non-agricultural societies increased in all the years during 1960-61 to 1980-81. It may be seen from the table that total advances of all the societies amounted to Rs. 3112 Lakhs in 1960-61. The amount increased to Rs. 27100 Lakhs in 1980-81. So it is evident that cooperative played some part in providing credit to the rural poor and to make themselves free to some extent from the clutches of the private money-lenders.

Together with credit created by commercial banks the total institutional credit available to the rural sector might be estimated at Rs. 790 crores. Total cropped area in West Bengal for 1978-79 is about 7 million hectares.[2] Modern technology requiring appropriate combination of fertilisers, water and insecticide chemicals has manifold increased the credit needs of agriculture. As a result, the credit needs per cropped hectare may be roughly estimated at Rs. 2000.[3] Therefore the total credit requirement of West Bengal's agriculture may be estimated at (7 x Rs. 2000) million or Rs. 1400 crores per annum.

Table 4.3

Cooperative Movement in West Bengal

S. No.	*Types of Societies*	*1960-61*	*1970-71*	*1976-77*	*1977-78*	*1978-79*	*1979-80*	*1980-81*
III.	Working Capital							
	(Rupees in Lakhs)							
(a)	Credit Societies							
	1. State & Central Banks	1370	4287	14813	16901	22141	23649	25980
	2. Land Mortgaged Banks	68	1180	4232	5937	7972	8753	10331
	3. Agriculture	518	2256	7672	9948	12763	13583	12942
	4. Non-agriculture	3068	7602	11636	12604	13121	15362	15791
	Total Credit Societies	5024	15325	38353	45390	55997	61347	65044
(b)	Total Non-credit Societies	467	2047	7268	9357	9779	9397	9397
	Total Societies	5491	17372	45621	54747	65776	70744	74441

Table 4.4
Cooperative Movement in West Bengal

S. No.	Types of Societies	1960-61	1970-71	1976-77	1977-78	1978-79	1979-80	1980-81
IV.	Loans Advanced							
	(Rupees in Lakhs)							
(a)	Credit Societies							
	1. State & Central Banks	680	1451	11598	10932	11810	10048	11516
	2. Land Mortgaged Banks	21	248	1492	1925	1087	1948	1251
	3. Agriculture	331	573	5252	5176	6414	4283	3914
	4. Non-agriculture	2071	5365	7127	7854	8571	9565	9708
	Total Credit Societies	3103	7637	25469	25887	27882	25844	26389
(b)	Total Non-credit Societies	9	93	506	530	1434	711	711
	Total Societies	3112	7730	25975	26417	29316	26555	27100

Source: Registrar of Cooperative Societies, West Bengal.

If commercial banks and cooperative societies supply only Rs. 790 crores, the rest Rs. 610 crores is expected to flow from the Regional Rural Banks which started functioning since 1975.

REFERENCES

1. Economic Survey, 1982-83, Govt. of India, New Delhi.
2. Govt. of West Bengal, Statistical Handbook, 1979.
3. G.C. Mandal, M.G. Ghosh, Economics of Green Revolution, Asia Publishing House, Bombay, 1976, pp. 36 & 63-66. This estimate excludes the portion of self-finance and is based upon actual receipt of credit, making allowance for inflationary rise in price-level.

5

Case Studies of Regional Rural Banks

It has been examined in Chapter 3 that in spite of substantial expansion of the commercial banking system in the wake of nationalisation of many major commercial banks of the country, the social infrastructure of the rural economy was far below what was necessary for its reasonable growth. It was still a long way off the desirable goal of bringing together different constituents of the rural economy under an organised system, mobilizing the rural surpluses and filling the great gap between the need and supply of rural credit. The regional Rural Banks with a network of branches were expected to meet this objective by extending the facilities of an organised banking system to the remotest corners of the rural area specially covering the needs of the rural poor.

The purpose of this chapter is to evaluate the structure and functioning of the Regional Rural Banks of West Bengal in the light of the results of case studies of these banks.

Each of the seven Regional Rural Banks of West Bengal was supplied with a questionnaire which it had to answer. The answer were recorded to provide database for analysis incorporated in this chapter.

The earlier part of the case studies consists of a description of the socio-economic and ecological characteristics of the area of operation of each of the Regional Rural Bank. Its purpose is to provide some knowledge of the real situation that should guide investment programme.

The other part is devoted to analysis of data collected from the Regional Rural Banks. Its purpose is to throw light on the functioning of the individual Regional Rural Bank. Data which have been used in this connection are related to progress of deposits and advances, business-behaviour as reflected in the profit or loss, composition of deposits, loaning operations, recovery of loans, progress in average deposit and advances per branch and also credit-deposit ratio per branch. It may be noted here that the nomenclature of the Regional Rural Banks reporting includes terms in the statement of their loaning operations, such as 'loans', 'advances', 'disbursements' and 'outstanding credit' which require precise definitions. The term 'advances' is used to imply cumulative total of loans from past years reduced by amounts of recovery plus interest and other charges every year. 'Disbursement of loans' implies loans made during the current year. 'Outstanding credit' is credit related to the current year. 'Outstanding credit' of the current year implies 'outstanding credit' of the previous year plus disbursement of loans of the current year minus debts and interest repaid during the current year on a particular date. This is same as "advances". Advances and disbursements are obviously different as explained above.

An explanation of the technique used in analysis of deposits and advances per branch is perhaps necessary.

All the branches of a Regional Rural Bank have been grouped according to the year of their start. For each group average deposits and average advances of the current year have been estimated by dividing the aggregate by the number of branches in the group.

This enables us to assess progress of an average branch in respect of deposits and advances with the passage of time. Such an assessment for an average branch is distinguished from the overall assessment of progress of the Regional Rural Bank as a whole. An overall progress may be simply due to multiplication of branches which may not reflect the efficiency of performance of a branch. The efficiency of performance of an average branch is better understood by subjecting the average deposits and advances of the branches of different age-groups to a scrutiny. The importance of this analysis will be more evident when a comparative assessment of the performances of the Regional Rural Bank is attempted. Some features common to all the RRBs, such as those relating to the rates of interest and mode of loaning operations are discussed in Chapter VI.

Also, the expenditure of the RRBs which are given here in abstract will be probed in further breakdowns, such as establishment and interest costs in Chapter 7.

1. MAYURAKSHI GRAMIN BANK

The area of operation of Mayurakshi Gramin Bank is Birbhum district. Total population of Birbhum district is 20,94,756. Total rural population is 19,20,229 comprising 91.67% of the total population. Total main workers are 5,88,622 in number of whom cultivators are 2,23,505, agricultural labourers are 2,25,930, household industry workers are 21,911 and other workers are 1,17,276 and percentages of cultivators, agricultural labourers, household industry workers and other workers to total workers are 37.97%, 38.38%, 3.72% and 19.93% respectively.[1]

Area of the district is 4550 sq. kms.[2] Annual rainfall is 1923.9 milimetres. In 1978-79 area of rice cultivation is 325.2 thousand hectares. Production of rice is 580.4 thousand tonnes. Yield is 1785 kgs. per hectare. Area of wheat cultivation is 56.8 thousand hectares. Production of wheat is 97.4 thousand tonnes. Yield is 1715 kgs. per hectare. Area of production of other cereals is 1.3 thousand hectares. Production of other cereals is 0.6 thousand tonnes. Yield is 462 kgs. per hectare. Area under pulses is 30.9 thousand hectares production of pulses is 10.9 thousand tonnes. Yield is 353 kgs. per hectare.

Average population per branch of commercial bank in the district is 26,000.[3]

There are seven towns in the district. Each of the four towns has a branch of Mayurakshi Gramin Bank. There are no branches in three towns. 15 branches were set up in 1981 in areas not specified as towns in the census of 1981.

Soil types of the district of Birbhum which is part of a laterite region are sandy clay loam and clay loam with concretion. In this region there is possibility of expansion of areas under fruits, flowers, timber, spices and medicinal plants.

Capital and Growth

Mayurakshi Gramin Bank was set up on 16th August, 1976 with its Head Office at Suri. It was sponsored by United Commercial Bank. The bank initiated its business with a paid up share capital of Rs. 25 Lakhs. The sponsoring bank contributed 35 per cent of its paid up share capital which amounted to Rs. 8.75 Lakhs. The Government of India contributed Rs. 12.50 Lakhs or 50 per cent of the total paid up capital, the remaining 15 per cent or Rs. 3.75 Lakhs was contributed by the Government of West Bengal. The authorised capital of the bank was fixed at Rs. 1 crore. The proportions of participation in the share capital of the bank were fixed by statutory provision.

Table MGB-1

Progress of Mayurakshi Gramin Bank during 1976-81

	1976	*1977*	*1978*	*1979*	*1980*	*1981*
Branches	8	14	24	26	35	50
Deposits	0.95	13.29	48.16	98.79	161.11	264.80
(Rs. Lakhs)		(1299)	(262)	(105)	(63)	(64)
Advances	0.18	31.89	63.12	112.76	142.82	282.15
(Rs. Lakhs)		(17617)	(98)	(79)	(27)	(98)
Income	0.95	5.24	7.40	10.73	18.17	25.33
(Rs. Lakhs)		(452)	(41)	(45)	(69)	(39)
Expenditure	0.69	6.39	12.14	15.72	24.07	38.18
(Rs. Lakhs)		(826)	(90)	(29)	(53)	(59)
Profit & Loss	(+) 0.26	(-) 1.15	(-) 4.74	(-) 4.99	(-) 5.90	(-) 12.85

(Figures in brackets are percentage increases over the previous years)

The progress of the bank in different respects is given in Table MGB-1. It is seen from the table that deposits of the bank increased from Rs. 0.95 Lakhs in 1976 to Rs. 13.29 Lakhs in 1977, Rs. 48.16 Lakhs in 1978, Rs. 98.79 Lakhs in 1979, Rs. 161.11 Lakhs in 1980 and Rs. 264.80 Lakhs in 1981. The increases in deposit over the previous years were 1299%, 262%, 105%, 63% and 64% respectively. The increases in advance over the previous years in the years 1977, 1978, 1979, 1980 and 1981 were by 17617%, 98%, 79%, 27% and 98% respectively.

The bank incurred loss in all the years as shown in Table MGB-1. The loss was due to lack of manpower planning and lack of proper economic or financial planning. Causes of the loss can be explained from income side and expenditure side. In income side ratio between investment of loanable fund and cost of fund was not maintained. Expenditure side consists of increased salary and wages to the staff and increased cost of inventories in relation to expansion of branches and volume of work. Another cause of loss is bad recovery performance which checked recycling of fund.

Composition of deposits of the bank according to their categories as given in Table MGB-2 shows that savings bank deposits were persistently predominant during all the six years constituting 84 per cent, 71 per cent, 75 per cent, 73 per cent, 72 per cent and 70 per cent respectively in the years 1976, 1977, 1978, 1979, 1980 and 1981. Time deposit was 27 per cent in 1977 but it declined to 22 per cent, 20 per cent, 20 per cent and 24 per cent respectively in the years 1978, 1979, 1980 and 1981. The bank was able to mobilize rural surpluses which is evident from the Table MGB-2.

Table MGB-2
Composition of Deposits by Category

Category	*1976 Amount Rs. Lakhs*	*1977 Amount Rs. Lakhs*	*1978 Amount Rs. Lakhs*	*1979 Amount Rs. Lakhs*	*1980 Amount Rs. Lakhs*	*1981 Amount Rs. Lakhs*
Fixed & Time	0.01	3.64	10.45	19.60	33.54	63.18
Deposits	(1)	(27)	(22)	(20)	(20)	(24)
Savings Bank	0.79	9.47	36.19	71.78	115.44	184.82
Deposits	(84)	(71)	(75)	(73)	(72)	(70)
Current Account	0.14	0.18	1.53	7.42	12.12	16.80
	(15)	(2)	(3)	(7)	(8)	(6)
Total	0.94	13.29	48.17	98.80	161.10	264.80
	(100)	(100)	(100)	(100)	(100)	(100)

According to the Annual Reports of the bank for the year 1979, 1980 and 1981 the bank borrowed Rs. 25 Lakhs from the Reserve Bank of India and Rs. 17.5 Lakhs from the United Commercial Bank under the refinance scheme for RRBs in 1979, Rs. 40 Lakhs from Reserve Bank of India and Rs. 17.50 Lakhs from United Commercial Bank were borrowed in 1980. In 1981 the bank borrowed Rs. 50 Lakhs from Reserve Bank of India and Rs. 63.43 Lakhs from the sponsor bank.

Loaning Operation

The major items of activities for which disbursement of loans of the bank were made from 1976 to 1981 were agriculture (short-term and medium-term): share croppers, marginal farmers and small farmers, non-agriculture (rural artisans, weavers, household crafts and industries, retailers and transport operators) and sericulture as shown in Table MGB-3. The table shows that the major part of the credit facilities of the bank was allocated to share croppers, marginal farmers and small farmers. Share croppers, marginal farmers and small farmers covered 72 per cent, 67 per cent, 54 per cent, 55 per cent and 48 per cent respectively in the years 1977, 1978, 1979, 1980 and 1981. Non-agricultural activities covered 16 per cent, 23 per cent, 24 per cent, 40 per cent and 52 per cent respectively in the years 1977, 1978, 1979, 1980 and 1981. Sericulture covered 12 per cent, 10 per cent, 22 per cent and 5 per cent respectively in the years 1977, 1978, 1979 and 1980. Increase in the share of non-agricultural activities during later years was rather commendable in view of the need of reducing excessive dependence on agriculture as a means of living.

Table MGB-3

Disbursement of Loans at Mayurakshi Gramin Bank

Items	*Amount of Loans Disbursed*											
	Rs. Lakhs	*%*	*Rs. Lakhs*	*%*	*Rs. Lakhs*	*%*	*Rs. Lakhs*	*%*	*Rs. Lakhs*	*%*	*Rs. Lakhs*	*%*
Agriculture (Short term and medium term): share croppers, marginal farmers and small farmers	0.18	100	23.03	72	42.30	67	29.33	54	42.16	55	92.20	48
Non-agriculture (rural artisans, weavers, household craft and industries retailers and transport operators)	–	5.11	–	16	14.82	23	12.97	24	31.00	40	100.05	52
Sericulture	–	3.93	–	12	6.00	10	12.00	22	4.00	5	–	–
Total	0.18	32.07			63.12		54.30		77.16		192.25	

Table MGB-4

Pattern of Outstanding Credit at Mayurakshi Gramin Bank

Item	*Account out-standing 1977 No. (%)*	*Amount out-standing 1977 Rs. Lakhs (%)*	*Account out-standing 1978 No. (%)*	*Amount out-standing 1978 Rs. Lakhs (%)*	*Account out-standing 1979 No. (%)*	*Amount out-standing 1979 Rs. Lakhs (%)*	*Account out-standing 1980 No. (%)*	*Amount out-standing 1980 Rs. Lakhs (%)*	*Account out-standing 1981 No. (%)*	*Amount out-standing 1981 Rs. Lakhs (%)*
Agriculture	4119 (74)	23.02 (82)	4236 (58)	36.24 (70)						
Non-agriculture	1428 (26)	5.11 (18)	3061 (42)	15.54 (30)						
Agriculture & Non-agriculture					9641 (100)	85.86 (100)	15667 (100)	142.85 (100)	25248 (100)	282.15 (100)
Total	5547 (100)	28.13 (100)	7297 (100)	51.78 (100)	9641 (100)	85.86 (100)	155667 (100)	142.85 (100)	25248 (100)	282.15 (100)

Note: Figures in parenthesis denote percentage.

A picture of the outstanding credit of Mayurakshi Gramin Bank at the end of December from 1977 to 1981 is presented in Table MGB-4.

In the year 1977 agricultural and non-agricultural activities covered 82 per cent and 18 per cent respectively of the total amount of outstanding credit spread over 74 per cent and 26 per cent respectively of the total borrower accounts. In the year 1978 while the share of agriculture in the total amount of outstanding credit fell to 70 per cent, that of the non-agricultural sector rose to 30 per cent. Their shares in the total number of accounts were 58 per cent and 42 per cent respectively, showing a remarkable shift in favour of the non-agricultural sector.

For later years figures were not available in separate breakdowns for the two sectors. However, both the total amount of outstanding credit and the number of borrower accounts greatly increased during 1979-81 as is evident from Table MGB-4.

Staffing Pattern and Training

The staff strength during the year 1981 was as follows:

(i)	Officer	45
(ii)	Senior Clerk-cum-Cashier	29
(iii)	Steno Typist-cum-Clerk	01
(iv)	Typist-cum-Clerk	01
(v)	Junior Clerk-cum-Field Assistant/Junior Field Assistant-cum-Clerk	79
(vi)	Messenger-cum-Sweeper/Sweeper	53

The staff members who received training from different institutions during the year 1981 is given below.

Categories of employees	*Number of employees/ officers trained*	*Course conducted by*	*Duration of training*
1.a) Branch manager	14	C.A.B. Pune Reserve Bank of India	Four weeks
b) Branch manager	15	On the job training in the bank	
2. Senior Clerk-cum-cashier	29	The Bank and the sponsor bank	One week
3.a) Junior Cler-cum-field assistant/ Junior Field Assistant-cum-Clerk	46	The Bank and the sponsor Bank	One week
b) Junior Clerk-cum-Field Assistant/Junior Field Assistant-cum-Clerk	32	On the job training in the Bank.	

Branches

During 1976 there were 8 branches of Mayurakshi Gramin Bank. The number of branches rose to 50 by 1981. Total rural population living in the area of operation of the bank is 19,20,229 (census of 1981). If one branch is required for every 50,000 of population then the number of branches should be 38. There were 50 branches in 1981. So branch expansion of the bank is satisfactory in the sense that a large number of rural people were being covered by the bank.

Average Amount of Deposit and Advances Per Branch

Table MGB-5 shows average amount per branch of deposits and advances of the branches of the bank grouped according to the year of their start. Both the average amount of deposits and advances per branch sharply increased during the course of 4 years of the

Mayurakshi Gramin Bank, though the increase was relatively slow during the first two years.

Table MGB-5
Average Amount of Deposit and Advances Per Branch of Mayurakshi Gramin Bank as in 1981

Year of Start	*Average deposit per branch (Rs. 1000)*	*Average advances per branch (Rs. 1000)*
1977	1052	1024
1978	668	603
1979	440	741
1980	381	655
1981	0.99	312

Table MGB-6
Credit Deposit Ratio for Branches as in 1981 by Year of Start

Year of Start	*Credit Deposit Ratio*
1977	1.15
1978	0.90
1979	1.68
1980	1.71
1981	3.15

It is seen that for the branches born in 1980 and 1981 the credit deposit ratios were much higher than that for branches born in 1977, 1978 and 1979. It appears that the growth of credit failed to match the growth of deposits in the case of Mayurakshi Gramin Bank during the 4 years course of its career.

2. GAUR GRAMIN BANK

The area of operation of Gaur Gramin Bank consists of three districts, namely, Malda, Murshidabad and West Dinajpur. Total population of Malda district is 20,35,009. Total rural population is 19,37,814 comprising of 95.22% of total population. Total main workers are 5,54,134 in number of whom cultivators are 2,21,911. Agricultural labourers are 1,90,606, household industry workers are 24,492 and other workers are 1,17,125 and percentages of cultivators, agricultural labourers, household industry workers and other workers to total workers 40.05%, 34.40%, 4.42% and 21.13% respectively.[4]

Area of the district is 3713 sq. kms.[5] Annual rainfall is 1558.4 mm. According to the statistics of 1978-79 area under rice cultivation is 211.8 thousand hectares. Production of rice is 234.1 thousand tons and yield is 1105 kgs. per hectare. Area under wheat is 34.5 thousand hectares. Production is 62.1 thousand tons and yield is 1801 kgs. per hectare. Area under other cereals is 23.4 thousand hectares. Production is 17.6 thousand tons and yield is 752 kgs. per hectare. Area under pulses is 63.2 thousand hectares. Production is 33.4 thousand tons and yield is 528 kgs. per hectare.

Average population per branch of commercial bank is 42,000.

There are eight towns in Malda district according to Census definition of 1981. Only one of these has a branch of Gaur Gramin Bank. Out of 22 branches 21 are located at places not enlisted as towns in the census.

Total population of Murshidabad district is 37,02,869. Total rural population is 33,58,490 which comprises 90.70% of total population. Total main workers is

9,89,423 of which cultivators are 3,48,190. Agricultural labourers are 3,33,494, household industry workers are 57,704 and percentages of cultivators, agricultural labourers, household industry workers and other workers to total workers are 35.19%, 33.71%, 5.83% and 25.27% respectively.

Area of the district is 5341 sq. kms. Annual rainfall is 1613.7 mm. In 1978-79 area under rice cultivation is 211.7 thousand hectares. Production is 553.7 thousand tons and yield is 1671 kgs. per hectare. Area under wheat is 111.6 thousand hectares. Production is 217.3 thousand tons and yield is 1947 kgs. per hectare. Area under other cereals is 14.7 thousand hectares. Production is 14.5 thousand tons and yield is 986 kgs. per hectare. Area under pulses is 115.4 thousand hectares. Production is 62.4 thousand tons and yield is 541 kgs. per hectare.

Average population per branch of commercial bank is 44000.

Number of towns in the district according to the census definition of 1981 is 14. All the 17 branches of the bank are located outside these towns.

Total population of West Dinajpur is 24,02,763. Total rural population is 21,35,206 which comprises 88.86% of total population. Total main workers are 7,17,225 in number of whom cultivators are 3,38,383, agricultural labourers are 2,45,709, household industry workers are 14,934 and other workers are 1,18,199 and percentages of cultivators, agricultural labourers, household industry workers and other workers to total workers are 47.18%, 34.26%, 2.08% and 16.48% respectively.

Area of the district is 5206 square kms. Annual rainfall is 2017.5 mm. In 1978-79 area under rice cultivation is 385.8 thousand hectares. Production is 385.0

thousand tons. Yield is 998 kgs. per hectare. Area under wheat is 51.5 thousand hectares. Production is 98.1 thousand tons. Yield is 1905 kgs. per hectare. Area under other cereals is 7.6 thousand hectares. Production is 5.4 thousand tons. Yield is 711 kgs. per hectare. Area under pulses is 46.6 thousand hectares. Production is 20.3 thousand tons. Yield is 436 kgs. per hectare.

Average population per branch of commercial bank is 50000.[6]

There are 8 towns in West Dinajpur according to census definition of 1981. One of the 13 branches of the bank in the district is located in one of these towns, rest being located outside the urban area.

Of the three districts constituting the area West Dinajpur belongs to the Hilly-terrain having all the agronomic and ecological characteristics of this region. The districts of Malda and Murshidabad are part of the alluvial region of the state comprising such soil type as loam, sandy loam, clay loam and sandy clay loam. The region is more or less normal in nutrient content. In addition to rice, jute, wheat, potato, pulses, onion, oil seeds, vegetables and bororice, some perennial crops like sugarcane, betel leaf, mango, guava and other fruits are also grown in the area.

Capital and Growth

Gaur Gramin Bank was one of the first five Regional Rural Banks in India and the only one in the Eastern Region. It was established on 2nd October, 1975 and was sponsored by the United Bank of India with its head office in Malda. The sponsoring bank contributed 35 per cent of its paid up share capital amounting to

Table GGB-1

Progress of Gaur Gramin Bank

	1975	*1976*	*1977*	*1978*	*1979*	*1980*	*1981*
Branches	2	22	30	31	33	39	56
Deposits	0.62	32.19	92.55	142.17	161.69	261.25	438.75
(Rs. Lakhs)		(5091)	(188)	(54)	(14)	(62)	(68)
Advances	1.61	105.99	235.88	348.46	464.68	414.25	553.47
(Rs. Lakhs)		(6483)	(123)	(48)	(33)	(–11)	(31)
Income	0.41	6.44	20.03	30.95	41.38	52.45	69.27
(Rs. Lakhs)		(1470)	(211)	(55)	(34)	(27)	(32)
Expenditure	0.14	6.90	19.15	27.25	35.83	51.32	71.41
(Rs. Lakhs)		(4829)	(178)	(42)	(31)	(43)	(39)
Profit and Loss	(+) 0.22	(–) 0.46	(+) 0.88	(+) 3.70	(+) 5.55	(+) 1.13	(–) 2.14

(Figures in brackets are percentage increases over the previous years)

Rs. 8.75 Lakhs. The Government of India contributed 50 per cent or Rs. 12.50 Lakhs of the total paid up share capital, the rest 15 per cent or Rs. 3.75 Lakhs was contributed by the Government of West Bengal. The authorised capital of the bank is fixed at Rs. 1 crore. The proportions of participation in the share capital of the bank are fixed by statutory provision.

The progress of the bank in different respects is shown in Table GGB-1. It is seen from the table that deposits of the bank increased from Rs. 0.62 Lakhs in 1975 to Rs. 30.19 in 1976, Rs. 92.55 Lakhs in 1977, Rs. 142.17 Lakhs in 1978, Rs. 161.69 Lakhs in 1979, Rs. 261.25 Lakhs in 1980 and Rs. 438.75 Lakhs in 1981. The advances also increased sufficiently in different years. The increases over the previous years were 6483 per cent, 123 per cent, 48 per cent, 33 per cent, and 31 per cent in the years 1976, 1977, 1978, 1979 and 1981 respectively.

In 1980 the advances decreased over the previous years by 11 per cent. It is known from the head office of the bank that the bank borrowed from Reserve Bank of India Rs. 10 Lakhs, 73.10 Lakhs, 104.45 Lakhs, 147.80 Lakhs, 180 Lakhs and 210 Lakhs in the years 1976, 1977, 1978, 1979, 1980, 1981 respectively. It borrowed from Agricultural Refinance and Development Corporation Rs. 2.21 Lakhs in 1979, 1.81 Lakhs in 1980 and 1.41 Lakhs in 1981. The bank borrowed from United Bank of India Rs. 50 Lakhs, 60 Lakhs, 73.30 Lakhs, 103.46 Lakhs, 128 Lakhs and 148 Lakhs in the year 1976, 1977, 1978, 1979, 1980 and 1981 respectively.

Composition of deposits of the bank according to their categories as given in Table GGB-2 shows that fixed deposits were subject to a trend of decline from a position of predominance (51.4% of the total deposits in 1976 and 45.8% in 1977) to a meagre position represented by the proportions of 14 per cent in 1980 and 17 per cent in 1981. While the proportion of Fixed Deposits diminished at an increasing rate, the proportion of Savings Account Deposits sharply increased from 24.7 per cent of 1976 to 62 per cent of 1981. It seems that there was a high degree of substitution of Savings Account Deposits for Fixed Deposits, revealing higher liquidity preference in the economy of the area in question. However, there was no denying the fact that the mobilization of rural savings in the area through the Regional Rural Bank was on the way to success.

The bank earned profit in the years 1975, 1977, 1978, 1979, 1980 which implies better monitoring and administrative efficiency on the part of the bank.

Loaning Operation

Amount of loans disbursed by the bank is shown in Table GGB-3. In 1975, 94 per cent of the total loan was disbursed to agriculture (direct) short term and medium term: share croppers, marginal farmers and small farmers and 6 per cent for other purposes. Of the total amount of loans 22%, 36%, 46%, 67% and 74% were disbursed in the short-term and medium term in the years 1977, 1978, 1979, 1980 and 1981 respectively. 59%, 47%, 39%, 11% and 8% of the total loans were disbursed to agriculture (indirect) in the years 1977, 1978, 1979, 1980 and 1981 respectively.

Community irrigation schemes received 10%, 6% and 2% of the total disbursement in the years 1977, 1978 and 1979 respectively. Shares of Agro-service-Unit were respectively 2%, 12% and 12% in the years 1977, 1980

Table GGB-2

Composition of Deposits by Category

	1976		1977		1978		1979		1980		1981	
	Amount Rs. lakhs	*% to total Deposits*	*Amount Rs. lakhs*	*% to total Deposits*	*Amount Rs. lakhs*	*% to total Deposits*	*Amount Rs. lakhs*	*% to total Deposits*	*Amount Rs. lakhs*	*% to total Deposits*	*Amount Rs. lakhs*	*% to total Deposits*
Current A/c.	1.49	4	1.94	2.1	1.33	.9	6.14	4	21.06	8	14.57	3
S.B. A/c.	9.15	24.7	27.07	29.3	63.13	44.4	86.71	54	146.40	56	272.44	62
R.D. A/c.	0.10	0.3	1.34	1.4	3.36	2.4	6.09	4	9.93	4	16.84	4
F.D. A/c.	19.01	51.4	42.38	45.8	53.77	37.8	35.19	22	36.58	14	72.56	17
Cash Certificate	0.12	0.3	3.27	3.5	6.86	4.8	-	-	18.39	7	27.46	6
Other Deposits	7.12	19.3	16.54	17.9	13.71	9.7	13.69	8	28.89	11	34.88	8
Contingent	-	-	-	-	-	-	13.88	-	-	-	-	-
Total	36.99	100	92.54	100	142.16	100	161.69	100	261.25	100	438.75	100

Table GGB-3

Disbursement of Loans at Gaur Gramin Bank

Items	*Amount of Loans Disbursed (Amount in Lakhs)*						
	1975	*1976*	*1977*	*1978*	*1979*	*1980*	*1981*
A. Agriculture (Direct)	1.37		53.41	39.93	53.62	66.69	163.58
Short-term and	(94)		(22)	(36)	(46)	(67)	(74)
Medium-term: share croppers,							
marginal farmers & small farmers							
B. Agriculture (Indirect)							
i) Short-term			128.21	46.27	38.29	—	—
ii) Medium term			12.01	6.32	6.86	11.31	18.01
			140.22	52.59	45.15		
			(59)	(47)	(39)	(11)	(8)
C. Community Irrigation Schemes			22.63	6.20	2.00		
(through Cooperative societies and			(10)	(6)	(2)		
C.A.D.P.)							

D. Agro-Service Unit							
i) Medium term			3.47	.37	—	12.14	26.12
ii) Cash Credit			1.27	0.00	—	(12)	(12)
			4.74				
			(2)				
E. Other Direct Loans							
i) Rural Artisans and SSI			4.56	2.77	2.76	5.76	11.05
						(6)	(6)
ii) Small business			5.71	6.42	8.46		
iii) Road Transport			2.71	1.88	1.83		
			12.98	11.97	13.05		
			(6)	(10)	(11)		
F. Others		0.09	1.90	1.66	2.40	3.36	
		(6)	(1)	(1)	(2)	(3)	
Total	1.46		235.88	111.82	116.22	99.22	218.76
	(100)		(100)	(100)	(100)	(100)	(100)

(Figures in brackets are percentages to total).

and 1981. Shares of rural artisans, small scale industries and road transport taken together were 6%, 10%, 11%, 6% and 6% respectively in the years 1977, 1978, 1979, 1980 and 1981.

Recovery Performance

Table GGB-4 shows that during 1980 recoveries of short-term agricultural loans, medium term agricultural loans and loans to artisans and small scale industries were to the extent of 47 per cent, 49 per cent and 63 per cent respectively of the total demand.

During 1981 recoveries rose to 53% in the case of short-term agricultural loans and 61% in the case of medium term agricultural loans. The recovery of loans in the case of artisans and small scale industries was to the extent of 62.27% during 1981. Thus the trend of recovery of loans appeared to the promising though there is much scope of improvement.

Staffing Pattern and Training

The staff strength as at the end of December, 1981 stood as below:

1.	Officers	67
2.	Field Investigators	62
3.	Senior Clerks	17
4.	Junior Clerks	72
5.	Driver	1
	Total	219

Manager (Development), Manager (Advance) and

Table GGB-4
Recovery Performance

Category of Loans	*Demand (Rs. Lakhs)*		*Recovery*			
			30 June 1980		*30 June 1981*	
	30 June 1980	*30 June 1981*	*Rs. Lakhs*	*Per cent*	*Rs. Lakhs*	*Per cent*
Agriculture						
A. Short-term	258.84	321.79	121.94	47.11	171.05	53.15
B. Mid-term	83.25	139.06	40.89	49.12	85.25	61.3
Artisan & SSI	9.70	13.65	6.08	62.68	6.50	62.27
Service Sector	21.52	33.01	15.77	73.28	25.49	77.22
Others	–	3.12	–	–	2.52	80.77

Manager (Inspection) were given one month's training at College of Agricultural Banking, Pune, other staff received no training.

Branches

The branches of the bank increased from 2 in 1975 to 56 in 1981.

Average Amount of Deposit and Advances Per Branch

Table GGB-5 shows average amount per branch of deposits and advances of the branches of the bank grouped according to the year of their start.

Table GGB-5
Average Amount of Deposit and Advances Per Branch of Gaur Gramin Bank as in 1981

Year of Start	*Average deposit per branch (Rs. 1000)*	*Average advances per branch (Rs. 1000)*
1976	1284	3320
1977	839	1353
1979	245	694
1980	421	580
1981	108	856

On the average a branch experienced a sharp rise both in its deposits and advances in the fourth year of its career. The rise in advances per branch was quite sharp in the fifth year.

Table GGB-6 clearly indicates that the credit-deposit ratio per branch was high irrespective of year of start. This implies that in the initial year deposit-mobilization per branch lagged far behind issue of credit largely supported by external sources. The credit-deposit-ratio for an average branch which completed five years of working is an evidence of both high degree of deposit mobilization and credit utilization.*

Table GGB-6
Credit Deposit Ratios for Branches as in 1981 by Year of Start

Year of Start	*Credit Deposit Ratio*
1976	2.59
1977	1.61
1979	2.83
1980	1.38
1981	7.93

* Cf. Chapter 7.

3. UTTARBANGA KSHETRIYA GRAMIN BANK

The area of operation of the Uttarbanga Kshetriya Gramin Bank comprises three districts of Cooch Behar, Jalpaiguri and Darjeeling. Total population of Cooch Behar district is 17,71,562. Total rural population is 16,19,222 comprising 93.9% of total population. Total main workers are 5,11,753 of which cultivators are 2,67,521. Agricultural labourers are 1,38,015, household industry workers are 12,064 and other workers are 94,153 and percentages of cultivators, agricultural labourers, household industry workers and other workers to total workers are 52.28%, 26.97%, 2.36% and 18.39% respectively.[7]

Area of the district is 3386 square kms.[8] Annual rainfall is 2504.3 mm. According to the statistics of 1978-79, area under rice cultivation is 260.8 thousand hectares.

Production of rice is 239.9 thousand tons. Yield is 920 kgs. per hectare. Area under wheat is 48.7 thousand hectares. Production of wheat is 103.6 thousand tonnes. Yield is 2127 kgs. per hectare. Area under other cereals is 2.5 thousand hectares. Production of other cereals is 0.7 thousand tonnes. Yield is 280 kgs. per hectare. Area under pulses is 15.0 thousand hectares. Production of pulses is 7.2 thousand tonnes. Yield is 480 kgs. per hectare.

Average Population per branch of commercial bank is 42000.[9]

There are eight towns in Cooch Behar district according to census definition of 1981. Only 2 of 19 branches of Uttarbanga Kshetriya Gramin Bank of the district are located each in two of these towns, rest being located at places which do not conform to the definition of towns.

Total population of Jalpaiguri district is 22,07,087. Total rural population is 18,96,241 comprising 85.92% of total population. Total main workers is 7,00,572 of which cultivators are 2,33,811, agricultural labourers are 1,11,243, household industry workers are 10,423 and other workers are 3,45,095 and percentages of cultivators, agricultural labourers, household industry workers and other workers to total workers are 33.37%, 15.88%, 1.49% and 49.26% respectively.

Area of the district is 6245 sq. kms. Annual rainfall is 3480.4 mm. According to the statistics for 1978-79 area under rice cultivation is 230.2 thousand hectares. Production of rice is 224.3 thousand tonnes. Yield is 974 kgs. per hectare. Area under wheat is 34.2 thousand hectares. Production is 60.1 thousand tonnes. Yield is 1726 kgs. per hectare. Area under other cereals is 5.0

thousand hectares. Production is 2.7 thousand tonnes. Yield is 450 kgs. per hectare. Area under pulses is 13.0 thousand hectares. Production is 5.4 thousand tonnes. Yield is 415 kgs. per hectare.

Average population per branch of commercial bank is 36000. In Jalpaiguri district there are 13 towns according to the census definition of 1981, 2 of which have each a branch of rural bank. Other 21 branch banks out of 23 in all are located at places other than towns.

Total population of Darjeeling district is 10,06,434. Total rural population is 7,26,062 comprising 72.14% of total population. Total main workers are 3,51,462 in number of whom cultivators are 9,4635, agricultural labourers are 30,848, household industry workers are 7,208, and other workers are 2,18,771 and percentages of cultivators, agricultural labourers, household industry workers and other workers to total workers are 26.93%, 8.78%, 2.05% and 62.24% respectively.

Area of the district is 3075 sq. kms. Annual rainfall is 3025.4 mm. According to 1978-79 statistics area under rice cultivation is 36.8 thousand hectares. Production is 38.8 thousand tonnes. Yield is 1054 kgs. per hectare. Area under wheat is 4.2 thousand hectares, production is 6.2 thousand tonnes, yield is 1483 kgs. per hectare. Area under other cereals is 33.3 thousand hectares. Production is 45.4 thousand tonnes. Yield is 136 kgs. per hectare. Area under pulses is 1.5 thousand hectares. Production is 1.0 thousand tonnes. Yield is 667 kgs. per hectare.

Average Population per branch of commercial bank is 14000.

There are 6 towns in Darjeeling district according

to census definition of 1981. Only one of 15 branch Rural Banks of the district is located in one of these towns, rest being located at places not recognised as towns.

The three districts of Cooch Behar, Jalpaiguri and Darjeeling belong to hilly terrain and share in its ecological characteristics. Soil types of the area are loam, sandy loam and clay loam. In addition to the usual cereals and pulses, some peculiar crops such as tobacco, pine apple, tea, litchi, mango, medicinal plants, oranges areconut and betel leaf are also grown in this area.

Capital and Growth

Uttarbanga Kshetriya Gramin Bank was established on 7th March, 1977 with its head office in Cooch Behar. The bank was sponsored by Central Bank of India. The sponsoring bank contributed 35 per cent of its paid up share capital amounting to Rs. 8.75 Lakhs. The Government of India contributed 50 per cent or Rs. 12.50 Lakhs of the total paid up share capital, the remaining 15 per cent or Rs. 3.75 Lakhs was contributed by the Government of West Bengal. The authorised capital of the bank is fixed at Rs. 1 crore. The proportions of participation in the share-capital of the bank are fixed by statutory provision.

The progress of the bank in different respects is shown in Table UBKGB-1. It may be seen from the table that deposits of the bank increased considerably from Rs. 1.26 Lakhs in 1977 to 2.06 Lakhs in 1978, 7.30 Lakhs in 1979, 63.64 Lakhs in 1980 and 200 Lakhs in 1981. The percentages of increase over the previous years are 63,254, 771, 214 respectively in the years 1978, 1979, 1980 and 1981. The advances were Rs. 3.27 Lakhs in

1977, 6.72 Lakhs in 1978, 10.27 Lakhs in 1979, 68.07 Lakhs in 1980 and 266.00 Lakhs in 1981. The advances also increased sufficiently in different years representing an increase of 106 per cent in 1978, 53 per cent in 1979, 563 per cent in 1980 and 291 per cent in 1981 over the respective previous years. The bank earned profit in the years 1977, 1978 and in 1979 and it incurred losses in 1980 and 1981.

It is known from the Annual Report of the bank that it borrowed Rs. 17200.00 from the Central Bank of India in 1979 and it borrowed Rs. 54.70 Lakhs from the Reserve Bank of India in 1980. According to the Annual Report of the Bank for the year 1981 the total amount of borrowing of the bank was Rs. 176.25 Lakhs of which Rs. 75 Lakhs was borrowed from Reserve Bank of India, Rs. 51.50 Lakhs from Central Bank of India, Rs. 37.62 Lakhs from Central Bank of India (D.R.I. refinance scheme), Rs. 12.13 Lakhs from Agricultural Refinance and Development Corporation.

Composition of deposits of the bank according to their categories as given in Table UBKGB-2 shows that Savings Bank deposits were persistently predominant constituting 94 per cent, 82 per cent and 77 per cent respectively in the years 1979, 1980 and 1981. In 1981 proportional increase in term deposits were greater than that for Savings Account Deposits, showing favourable trend in the mobilization of rural savings.

Loaning Operation

Amount of loans disbursed by the bank is shown in Table UBKGB-3. In 1979 the bank provided credit to agriculture (short-term and medium-term); share croppers, small farmers and marginal farmers, rural

Table UBKGB-1

Progress of Uttarbanga Kshetriya Gramin Bank during 1977-81

	1977	*1978*	*1979*	*1980*	*1981*
Branches	2	2	10	39	57
Deposits	1.26	2.06	7.30	63.64	200.00
(Rs. Lakhs)		(63)	(254)	(771)	(214)
Advances	3.27	6.72	10.27	68.07	266.00
(Rs. Lakhs)		(106)	(53)	(563)	(291)
Income	1.24	2.54	2.88	6.20	22.25
(Rs. Lakhs)		(105)	(14)	(115)	(259)
Expenditure	0.49	0.80	2.13	14.69	36
(Rs. Lakhs)		(163)	(167)	(591)	(145)
Profit & Loss	(+) 0.75	(+) 1.75	(+) 0.76	(–) 8.49	(–) 13.75
Recovery Performance	68.58%	59.11%	70.50%	60.63%	68.11%

(Figures in brackets are percentages increases over the previous years)

artisans and small scale industries, small business, self-employment and retail trade the percentage shares of which were 84, 1 and 15 respectively.

Table UBKGB-2
Composition of Deposits by Category

Category	*1979 Amount (Rs. Lakhs)*	*1980 Amount (Rs. Lakhs)*	*1981 Amount (Rs. Lakhs)*
Savings Bank Account	6.67	52.12	153.05
	(94)	(82)	(77)
Term Deposit	0.37	9.21	41.21
	(5)	(14)	(20)
Current Account	0.04	2.31	5.74
	(1)	(4)	(3)
Total	7.08	63.64	200.00
	(100)	(100)	(100)

The pattern of credit-allocation for 1980 and 1981 showed a remarkable shift in favour of small business, self-employment and retail trade share of which rose to 50 per cent and 49 per cent respectively in these two later years. In 1979 major part of credit facility was allocated to agriculture. In 1980 and 1981 small business, self-employment and retail trade received top priority in respect of credit. Next in importance was agriculture.

A picture of the outstanding credit of Uttarbanga Kshetriya Gramin Bank at the end of December, 1981, presented in Table UBKGB-4 shows that agriculture commanded 42 per cent of the total amount of outstanding credit spread over 37 per cent of the borrower accounts and activities allied to agriculture in 1981. The borrower accounts of rural artisans, cottage industries and services were 61 per cent of the total embracing 57 per cent of the total amount of outstanding credit.

Table UBKGB-3
Disbursement of Loans at Uttarbanga Kshetriya Gramin Bank

Items	*Amount of loan disbursed*					
	1979		*1980*		*1981*	
	Rs. Lakh	*%*	*Rs. lakh*	*%*	*Rs. lakh*	*%*
Agriculture (short-term and medium term): share cropper, small farmers & marginal farmers	8.32	84	20.00	38	117.89	45
Rural artisans & small scale industries	0.14	1	0.92	2	5.25	2
Small business, self-employment and retail trade.	1.53	15	25.80	50	129.18	49
Road Transport			5.40	10	11.25	4
Total	9.99	100	52.12	100	263.57	100

Table UBKGB-4
Pattern of Outstanding Credit at Uttarbanga Kshetriya Gramin Bank

Items	*Accounts outstanding end of Dec. 1981*		*Amount outstanding end of Dec. 1981*	
	Number	*Percentage to total*	*Rs. lakhs*	*Percentage to total*
Agriculture:				
short-term	6285	26	25.06	9
mid & long-term	2651	11	28.78	11
Allied activities	3336		57.42	22
Total agriculture	12272	37	111.26	42

Non-Agriculture:				
Rural Artisans & Cottage Industries	494	14	6.05	2
Service	11322	47	146.45	55
Total: Non-agriculture	11816	61	152.50	57
Non Priority:				
House-building (Bank premises) Staff advance	106	2	2.15	1
Total	24194	100	265.91	100

Source: Annual Report of Uttarbanga Kshetriya Gramin Bank, 1981.

Staffing Pattern and Training

The total number of staff under different categories as on 31.12.1981 is given below:

1. Branch Manager/Manager	36
2. Field Supervisor	74
3. Clerk-cum-Cashier	132
4. Driver	1
5. Messenger	60
6. Deputed Officer	1
	277

The bank has taken up the matter of training with Central Bank of India, the sponsoring bank and it has been decided that faculty members of the Staff Training Centre, Calcutta, will come and impart training to the officers of this bank. The training will be imparted to the officers of the bank in two batches. After the training the bank will send some of its officers batch-wise to the College of Agricultural Banking, Pune, for further training. Under sponsorship of Agricultural Refinance and Development Corporation, three Field Supervisors have taken training at Cooperative Training Centre, Uttarpara, practical training on specific subjects are arranged at branches of Central Bank of India. Central Bank of India has been requested to arrange training of the staff of the bank at their Regional Staff Training Centre.

Branches

The branches of the bank increased from 2 in 1978 to 10 in 1979, representing an increase of 400 per cent in branch expansion. In 1980 branches increased to 39 indicating 790 per cent rise in branch expansion. In 1981 branches increased to 57 showing a rise in branch expansion by 46 per cent over the previous year. Total rural population living in the area of operation of the bank is 42,71,525 (census of 1981). If one branch is required for every 50,000 of population then the number of branches should rise to more than 85.

Recovery Performance

Recovery performance of the bank is promising in the context of the overall recovery position of the banking sector operating in the districts where Uttarbanga Kshetriya Gramin Bank is operating. The recoveries of old loans were 60.58 per cent, 59.11 per cent, 70.50 per cent, 60.63 per cent and 68.11 per cent respectively in the years 1977, 1978, 1979, 1980 and 1981. (Reference: Annual Report of the Bank).

Average Amount of Deposit and Advances Per Branch

Table UBKGB-5 shows average amount per branch of deposits and advances of the branches of the bank grouped according to the year of their start. Both the average amount of deposits and advances per branch sharply rose during the first two years of the life of a branch. A branch on the average appeared to have reached its peak in the second year of its career. The third year witnessed a decline.

Table UBKGB-5

Average Amount of Deposits and Advances Per Branch of Uttarbanga Kshetriya Gramin Bank as in 1981

Year of Start	*Average deposit per branch (Rs. 1000)*	*Average advances per branch (Rs. 1000)*
1978	310	696
1979	511	740
1980	388	473
1981	175	247

Table UBKGB-6

Credit Deposit Ratio for Branches as in 1981 by Year of Start

Year of Start	*Credit Deposit Ratio*
1978	2.25
1979	1.45
1980	1.22
1981	1.41

It is evident from Table UBKGB-6 that credit-deposit-ratio for the oldest branches was sharply higher than that for the younger ones. It is apparent from the case of Uttarbanga Kshetriya Gramin Bank that with maturity a branch was in a position to achieve more intensive utilization of credit.

4. MALLABHUM GRAMIN BANK

The area of operation of Mallabhum Gramin Bank consists of three districts namely, Bankura, Midnapore and Purulia. Total population of Bankura district is 23,74,205. Total rural population is 21,93,034 comprising 92.37% of total population. Total main workers are 6,89,863 of which cultivators are 2,83,463. Agricultural labourers are 2,36,917. Household industry workers are 34,569 and other workers are 1,34,914 and percentages of cultivators, agricultural labourers, household industry workers and other workers to total workers are 41.09%, 34.34%, 5.01% and 19.56% respectively.[10]

Area of the district is 6881 sq. kms.[11] Annual rainfall is 777.5 mm. In 1978-79 area under rice cultivation is 362.1 thousand hectares, production of rice is 512.3 thousand tonnes. Yield is 1415 kgs. per hectare. Area under wheat is 27.1 thousand hectares. Production of wheat is 45.9 thousand tonnes. Yield is 1694 kgs. per hectare. Area under other cereals is 2.4 thousand hectares. Production of other cereals is 3.4 thousand tonnes. Yield is 1417 kgs. per hectare. Area under pulses is 11.5 thousand hectares. Production of pulses is 4.8 thousand tonnes. Yield is 417 kg. per hectare.

Average population per branch of commercial bank is 36,000.[12]

There are five towns in Bankura district according to census definition of 1981. Only 2 of 27 branches of Mallabhum Gramin Bank of the district are located each in two of these towns, rest being located at places which do not conform to the definition of towns.

Total population of Midnapur district is 67,23,860. Total rural population is 61,49,843 comprising 91.46% of total population. Total main workers is 19,67,762 of which cultivators are 9,52,174, agricultural labourers are 5,52,601, household industry workers are 81,712 and other workers are 3,81,275 and percentages of cultivators, agricultural labourers, household industry workers and other workers to total workers are 48.39%, 28.08%, 4.15% and 19.38% respectively.

Area of the district is 13,724 sq. kms. Annual rainfall is 1390.6 mm. in 1978-79 area under rice cultivation is 884.4 thousand hectares. Production of rice is 1115.8 thousand tonnes. Yield is 1262 kgs. per hectare. Area under wheat is 24.7 thousand hectares. Production of wheat is 48.2 thousand tonnes. Yield is 1951 kgs. per hectare. Area under other cereals is 2.5 thousand hectares. Production of other cereals is 2.0 thousand tonnes. Yield is 800 kgs. per hectare. Area under pulses is 60.7 thouand hectares. Production of pulses is 26.0 thousand tonnes. Yield is 428 kgs. per hectare.

Average population per branch of commercial bank is 42,000.

There are 19 towns in the Midnapore district according to census definition of 1981. Only one of 28 branches of Mallabhum Gramin Bank is located in one town, the rest being located at places other than towns.

Total population of Purulia district is 18,55,429. Total rural population is 16,88,532 comprising 91% of total population. Total main workers is 5,76,709 of which cultivators are 2,90,975, agricultural labourers are 1,42,186, household industry workers are 20,215 and other workers are 1,23,333 and percentages of cultivators, agricultural labourers, household industry workers and other workers to total workers are 50.45%, 24.65%, 3.51% and 21.39% respectively.[1]

Area of the district is 6259 sq. kms.[2] Annual rainfall is 1447.9 mm. In 1978-79 area under rice cultivation is 245.7 thousand hectares. Production of rice is 286.4 thousand tonnes. Yield is 1166 kgs. per hectare. Area under wheat is 12.1 thousand hectares. Production of wheat is 20.1 thousand tonnes. Yield is 1658 kgs. per hectare. Area under other cereals is 10.0 thousand tonnes. Yield is 560 kgs. per hectare. Production is 5.6 thousand tonnes. Area under pulses is 16.4 thousand hectares. Production of pulses is 7.0 thousand tonnes. Yield is 427 kgs. per hectare.

Average population per branch of commercial bank is 30,000.

There are eight towns in Purulia district according to census definition of 1981. There are 13 branches of Mallabhum Gramin Bank in Purulia district. Only one branch is located in town and the rest are located at places other than towns.

Capital and Growth

Mallabhum Gramin Bank started business with a paid up share capital of Rs. 25 Lakhs. It was sponsored by the United Bank of India, contributing 35 per cent of its paid up share capital which amounted to Rs. 8.75 Lakhs. The Government of India contributed Rs. 12.50 Lakhs or 50 per cent of the total paid up capital, the rest (15 per cent) or Rs. 3.75 Lakhs came from the Government of West Bengal. The authorised capital of

Table MBGB-1

Progress of Mallabhum Gramin Bank during 1976-81

Items	*1976*	*1977*	*1978*	*1979*	*1980*	*1981*
No. of Branches	18	32	37	54	68	69
Deposits	8.43	72.69	181.25	364.70	530.66	701.08
(Rs. Lakhs)		(762)	(149)	(101)	(46)	(32)
Advances	5.39	63.32	127.34	214.43	372.07	453.63
(Rs. Lakhs)		(1074)	(101)	(68)	(74)	(22)
Income	1.96	8.01	17.86	32.88	56.52	81.02
(Rs. Lakhs)		(309)	(123)	(84)	(72)	(43)
Expenditure	2.10	10.51	19.47	31.71	54.96	78.22
(Rs. Lakhs)		(400)	(86)	(63)	(73)	(42)
Profit & Loss	(–) 0.14	(–) 2.50	(–) 1.61	(+) 1.17	(+) 1.56	(+) 2.80
(Rs. Lakhs)						

Source: Annual Reports, Mallabhum Gramin Bank and interview with the Chairman (Figures in brackets indicate percentage of increase over the previous years)

Table MBGB-2

Composition of Deposits by Category

Category	*1976 (Rs. Lakhs)*	*1977 (Rs. Lakhs)*	*1978 (Rs. Lakhs)*	*1979 (Rs. Lakhs)*	*1980 (Rs. Lakhs)*	*1981 (Rs. Lakhs)*
Fixed Deposit	2.48	25.71	57.11	93.66	137.00	189.21
	(29)	(35)	(32)	(26)	(26)	(27)
Savings Bank Deposits	5.39	43.80	110.23	222.14	322.61	428.77
	(64)	(60)	(61)	(61)	(61)	(61)
Current Account	0.55	3.19	13.91	48.91	71.05	82.10
	(7)	(5)	(8)	(13)	(13)	(12)
Total	8.42	72.70	181.25	364.71	530.66	700.08
	(100)	(100)	(100)	(100)	(100)	(100)

(Figures in the brackets indicate percentage of the total)

Table MBGB-3

Disbursement of Loans at Mallabhum Gramin Bank

Items	*Amount of Loans Disbursed*							
	1978		*1979*		*1980*		*1981*	
	Rs. Lakh	%	*Rs. Lakhs*	%	*Rs. Lakhs*	%	*Rs. Lakhs*	%
Agriculture (Short-term and medium term): share croppers, small farmers & marginal farmers.	46.72	60	93.08	64	98.71	52	69.48	64
Village and cottage industries.	3.48	4	7.28	5	10.67	6	4.76	4
Small business, self-employment and retail trade.	27.82	36	44.69	31	80.24	42	35.00	32
Total	78.02	100	145.05	100	189.62	100	109.24	100

the bank was fixed at Rs. 1 crore. The proportions of participation in the share-capital of the bank were fixed by statutory provision. According to the Annual Reports of the bank it borrowed Rs. 17 Lakhs, Rs. 125 Lakhs and Rs. 125 Lakhs from the Reserve Bank of India in the year 1979, 1980 and 1981 respectively. It borrowed from the sponsoring bank Rs. 11.90 Lakhs, 11.90 Lakhs and 11.90 Lakhs in the year 1979, 1980 and 1981 respectively. The bank borrowed from Industrial Development Bank of India Rs. 4.28 Lakhs, Rs. 8.79 Lakhs and Rs. 11.56 Lakhs in the year 1979, 1980 and 1981 respectively.

The progress of the bank in different respects is given in Table MBGB-1. It may be seen from the table that deposits of the bank sharply increased from Rs. 8.43 Lakhs of the initial year (1976) to Rs. 72.69 Lakhs in 1977. The increase was by 762 per cent or more than 8 times. In the course of one year between 1978 and 1979 it further increased by 149 per cent. The years 1979, 1980 and 1981 witnessed a rise of 101 per cent, 46 per cent and 19 per cent respectively. The advances of the bank also similarly increased by 1074 per cent, 101 per cent, 68 per cent, 74 per cent and 22 per cent respectively in 1977, 1978, 1979, 1980 and 1981 over the previous years. It may be seen that the rate of growth in both the cases of deposits and advances was tending to fall with the passage of years. Though in the initial two years the bank suffered considerable losses, in later three years it could earn profit to the extent of Rs. 1.17 Lakhs, Rs. 1.51 Lakhs and Rs. 2.80 Lakhs respectively. On the whole a judicious balance between increase in income and increase in expenditure was maintained so that the bank could build a reserve fund of Rs. 1.27 Lakhs in 1981. Thus the promise of success of the bank which was quite perceptible was inherent in sound management.

Composition of deposits of the bank according to their categories as given in Table MBGB-2 shows that deposits on savings bank account were persistently predominant during all the three years, constituting 61 per cent of the total in all the four years 1978, 1979, 1980 and 1981. It was 64 per cent and 60 per cent in the years 1976 and 1977 respectively. Next in importance was fixed deposit varying between 26 and 35 per cent of the deposits. According to the Annual Report of the Bank for 1980 average deposit per account worked out to Rs. 825 at the end of December 1980. It is, therefore, evident that the bank could be instrumental to mobilizing surpluses of rural households which emerged in the form of small savings. The working capital of the bank was also supplemented by borrowings from the Reserve Bank of India, United Bank of India and Industrial Development Bank of India which as of June 1981, stood at Rs. 12.50 million, Rs. 1.19 million and Rs. 9.4 Lakhs respectively.

Loaning Operations

The major items of activities for which the bank provided credit support in 1978, 1979, 1980 and 1981 were agriculture (short term and medium term): share-croppers, marginal farmers and small farmers, village and cottage industries, small business and self-employment as shown in Table MBGB-3.

The table indicates that the major part of the credit facilities of the bank was allocated to share-croppers, marginal farmers and small farmers covering around

60%, 64%, 52% and 64% respectively in the years 1978, 1979, 1980 and 1981.

A more detailed picture of the outstanding credit at the end of December 1980 is presented in Table MBGB-4. The share of agriculture in the total volume of credit was 59 per cent spread over 71 per cent of the total number of borrower accounts. The amount of outstanding agricultural loan was only Rs. 311/- per account. The share of small scale industries and artisans in the total volume of credit was rather small (6% of the total). It may be noted that the share of credit going to agriculture, though big, was much less than its share in the total number of workers which is around 77 per cent. Diversion of credit to non-agricultural activities has been partly due to limited scope of irrigation-development and associated multiple-cropping. There is a prima facie case, too, for the strengthening or development of non-agricultural activities which would relieve the pressure of excessive dependence on agriculture. It was, therefore, commendable that the bank provided in 1980 credit support for 5465 retail traders, 599 small-scale industrial units, 1274 self-employed persons, 625 road transport operators and 1569 artisans. (Table MBGB-4)

Some of the activities which the bank financed were under the purview of the projects of the Area Development Corporation. According to the Annual Report for 1980 loan in this category worked out to Rs. 15.56 Lakhs by the end of 1980. Further bank sanctioned loans for 405 dug wells in 1980 amounting to Rs. 10.15 Lakhs. In 1979, 1559 share-croppers and in 1980, 2345 share-croppers and allottees of vested lands were provided with credit to the tune of Rs. 3.03 Lakhs and Rs. 5.25 Lakhs respectively.

Table MBGB-4
Pattern of Outstanding Credit at Mallabhum Gramin Bank

Items	*Accounts outstanding end of Dec. 1981*		*Amount outstanding end of Dec. 1981*	
	Number	*Percentage to total*	*Rs. '000*	*Percentage to total*
Agriculture: (Direct)	16612	45	16559	44
Agriculture (Indirect)	9431	26	5546	15
Retail trade	5465	15	8046	22
Small-scale industries	599	2	1596	4
Self-employed persons	1274	3	1043	3
Road Transport	625	2	390	1
Artisans	1569	4	898	2
Others	1017	3	3151	9
Total	36592	100	37207	100

Source: Annual Report of Mallabhum Gramin Bank, 1980.

Recovery of Loans

While the recovery of non-agricultural loans by 1980 was to the tune of 65 per cent, the recovery of agricultural loans was sagging at 35 per cent (Annual Report for 1980). The overall recovery recorded 45 per cent of the total loans. Poor repayment performance for agricultural borrowers obviously warrants better care for the agricultural business so that its repayment capacity is increased. The success of a business is indicated by the repayment of loans advanced to it. It is necessary to develop a network of Farmers' Service Cooperative Societies which must be strong and effective. Moreover, teh existing primary Agricultural Credit Societies must be strengthened. If loans are channelled through and monitored by such societies, repayment performance can be expected to improve. What is necessary is not only the improvement of production technology improving the yield rate but also the improvement of the morale of the farming community. Unfortunately, only 47 primary societies have so far been ceded to the bank and 4 Farmers' Service Cooperative Societies have been organised to serve as agency for loaning operations of the Regional Rural Bank. It is desirable that the State Government should come forward with more positive encouragement for the promotion of the participation of the cooperatives in the loaning programmes of the bank. Another limitation of the loaning programme of a Regional Rural Bank is felt to be its restricted scope from which substantial farmers are excluded. But credit advanced to them could be a more profitable venture and return from it would have ultimately augmented the resources of the bank and their availability for rural poor.

Staffing Pattern and Training

At the end of 1980 the staff of the bank consisted of 55 Branch Managers, 27 Field Officers, 11 Officers, 4 Field Assistants, 2 Stenographers, 22 Senior Clerk-cum-Cashiers and 86 Junior Clerks.

To meet the need of trained personnel arrangements were made to provide training facilities for the staff of the bank. Branch Managers have been trained at the College of Agricultural Banking, Pune, in the administration of rural financing. In 1980 the staff-training college of the United Bank of India offered two courses specially for the officers of the Regional Rural Bank in which 31 members participated.

Branches

The number of branches of the bank went on increasing until at the end of 1981 it stood at 69. This implied that the number of branches increased by more than 100 per cent within four years. But even now the number of branches may not be considered adequate. The rural population living in the area of operation of the bank is 1,00,31,409 (census of 1981). If one branch is needed for every 50,000 of population, then the number of branches should rise to 168. In fact, the success of the rural banking system would very much depend upon network of branch banking. But the greatest limitation of branch expansion is dearth of trained personnel. Lack of proper houses is also a handicap. An appropriate and adequate training programme for staff of rural banks at all levels is an indispensable requirement for efficiency and success of the rural banking system.

Table MBGB-5
Average Amount of Deposits and Advances Per Branch of Mallabhum Gramin Bank as in 1981

Year of Start	*Average deposit per branch (Rs. 1000)*	*Average advances per branch (Rs. 1000)*
1976	1683	1062
1977	1330	919
1978	743	597
1979	547	555
1980	214	295
1981	115	31

Average Amount of Deposit and Advances Per Branch

Table MBGB-5 shows average amount per branch of deposits and advances of the branches of the bank grouped according to the year of start. It is seen from the table that deposits and advances per branch were steadily increasing as it was growing older.

Credit-Deposit Ratio

Table MBGB-6 indicates that for branches born in 1981 credit-deposit ratio is extremely low (0.26). It sharply rises to 1.37 with the passage of one year but falls to 0.69 for branches five year old.

Table MBGB-6
Credit Deposit Ratios of Branches as in 1981 by Year of Start

Year of Start	*Credit Deposit Ratio*
1976	0.63
1977	0.69
1978	0.80
1979	1.01
1980	1.37
1981	0.26

5. NADIA GRAMIN BANK

The area of operation of Nadia Gramin Bank is Nadia district. Total population of Nadia district is 29,77,013. Total rural population is 23,38,848 which comprises 78.56% of total population. Total number of main workers is 7,86,497 of which cultivators are 2,49,116, agricultural labourers are 2,25,197, household industry workers are

48,313 and other workers are 2,63,871 and percentages of cultivators, agricultural labourers, household industry workers are other workers to total workers are 31.67%, 28.63%, 6.14% and 33.56% respectively.[14]

Area of the District is 3926 sq. kms.[14] Annual rainfall is 1520.9 mm.

According to the statistics of 1978-79, area under rice is 195.0 thousand hectares. Production is 238.1 thousand tons and yield is 1221 kgs. per hectare. Area under wheat is 47.2 thousand hectares. Production is 97.2 thousand tons and yield is 2060 kgs. per hectare. Area under other cereals is 4.2 thousand hectares. Production is 3.0 thousand tons and yield is 714 kgs. per hectare. Area under pulses is 90.1 thousand hectares. Production is 39.1 thousand tons and yield is 434 kgs. per hectare.

Average population per branch of commercial bank is 30,000.[15]

There are twenty two towns in Nadia district according to the census definition of 1981. 12 branches of Nadia Gramin Bank were set up in 1981, one branch being located in town and the rest 11 branches in areas not specified as towns in census of 1981.

Nadia is a part of the alluvial region having all its ecological characteristics. Here in high and mid-land situations where if irrigation is available more lands can be put under wheat, pulses and oilseeds.

Capital and Growth

Nadia Gramin Bank was started on 27th August, 1980, with its head office at Krishnagar, Nadia. It was sponsored by United Bank of India. Nadia Gramin Bank started its business with a paid up share capital of Rs. 25 Lakhs. The sponsoring bank contributed 35 per cent of its paid up share capital which amounted to Rs. 8.75 Lakhs. The Government of India contributed Rs. 12.50 Lakhs or 50 per cent of the total paid up capital, the rest 15 per cent or Rs. 3.75 Lakhs was contributed by the Government of West Bengal. The authorised capital of the bank was fixed at Rs. 1 crore. The proportions of participation in the share capital of the bank were fixed by statutory provision.

The progress of the bank in various respects is given to Table NGB-1. It may be seen from the table that deposits of the bank increased considerably from Rs. 0.47 Lakhs in 1980 to Rs. 18.98 Lakhs in 1981. The increase was by 1938 per cent. In 1982 deposit further increased to 68.60 Lakhs. The increase was 261 per cent. The advances of the bank increased from Rs. 21.15 Lakhs in 1981 to 59.77 Lakhs in 1982. The increase in advances was by 182 per cent. The bank incurred losses in 1980, 1981 and 1982. The loss was due to increase in establishment cost on account of enhancement of salaries of staff and expenditure incurred during the initial period of its starting.

Composition of deposits of the bank according to their categories as given in Table NGB-2 shows that Savings Bank deposits were persistently predominant during all the three years constituting 92 per cent, 72 per cent and 60 per cent respectively in the years 1980, 1981 and 1982.

Time deposit increased from 8 per cent in 1980 to 23 per cent in 1981 but it declined to 9 per cent in 1982. Other deposits increased from 5 per cent in 1981 to 31 per cent in 1982. It is evident from Table NGB-2 that the bank was instrumental in mobilising surpluses of the rural households.

Table NGB-1

Progress of Nadia Gramin Bank during 1980-82

	1980	*1981*	*1982*
Branches	2	12	17
Deposits	0.47	18.98	68.60
(Rs. Lakhs)		(3938)	(261)
Advances	Nil	21.15	59.77
(Rs. Lakhs)			(183)
Income	0.86	4.72	9.77
(Rs. Lakhs)		(448)	(107)
Expenditure	0.90	5.39	13.52
(Rs. Lakhs)		(498)	(151)
Profit & Loss	(–) 0.04	(–) 0.67	(–) 3.75

(Figures in brackets are percentage increases over the previous years)

Table NGB-2

Composition of Deposits by Category

Category	*1980 Amount (Rs. Lakhs)*	*1981 Amount (Rs. Lakhs)*	*1982 Amount (Rs. Lakhs)*
Savings Bank	0.45	13.66	40.72
	(92)	(72)	(60)
Time Deposit	0.04	4.45	6.37
	(8)	(23)	(9)
Others	Nil	0.87	21.51
		(5)	(31)

(Figures in brackets are percentage to total.)

According to the Annual Report of the Bank for the year 1982, the bank borrowed Rs. 14 Lakhs from Reserve Bank of India/NABARD, Rs. 4.80 Lakhs from

United Bank of India and Rs. 0.51 Lakhs from ARDC/ NABARD. Its borrowings were nil in 1980 and 1981.

Loaning Operation

The items of activities for which the bank disbursed loans in 1981 and 1982 were agriculture (short-term and medium-term): share croppers, marginal farmers and small farmers, rural industries, transport, small business, consumption and others as shown in Table NGB-3. The table shows that the largest and major part of the credit facilities of the bank was allocated to agriculture, small business appearing next in importance. These two major items covered around 76 per cent and 18 per cent of the total loans in 1981. In 1982 the share of agriculture further rose to 80 per cent, while that of small business declined to around 14 per cent. The share of rural industries in both the years was around 2 per cent. There was no loaning operation in 1980.

A detailed picture of the outstanding credit of Nadia Gramin Bank at the end of December 1981 and 1982 is presented in Table NGB-4. Here again agriculture commanded most of the outstanding credit covering 69 per cent of the total amount spread over 87 per cent of the total borrower accounts in 1981. The share of agriculture in total oustanding credit rose to 82 per cent in 1982 spread over 85 per cent of the total accounts. The next in importance in this regard was the item "small business" covering 15 per cent of total amount spread over 8.6 per cent of the accounts in 1981. In 1982 the share of small business in total amount and total accounts fell to 13 per cent and 11 per cent respectively. The share of small-scale industries and artisans was rather dwindling.

Table NGB-3

Disbursement of Loans at Nadia Gramin Bank

Items	*Amount of Loans Disbursed*					
	1980		*1981*		*1982*	
	Rs. Lakh	%	*Rs. Lakhs*	%	*Rs. Lakhs*	%
Agriculture (Short-term and medium term): share-croppers, marginal farmers & small farmers.	Nil	—	16.12	76.21	44.47	80.45
Rural Industries	Nil	—	0.45	2.12	1.31	2.37
Transport Operators	Nil	—	0.05	0.24	0.48	0.86
Small Business	Nil	—	3.73	17.64	7.54	13.64
Consumption	Nil	—	0.01	0.04	—	—
Others	Nil	—	0.79	3.75	1.48	2.68
Total	Nil		21.15	100.00	55.28	100.00

Table NGB-4

Pattern of Outstanding Credit at Nadia Gramin Bank

Items	*Accounts Outstanding 1981*	%	*Amount Outstanding 1981 (Rs. Lakhs)*	%	*Accounts Outstanding 1982*	%	*Amount Outstanding 1982 (Rs. Lakhs)*	%
S.T.F.L.	149	70	0.950	64	4513	83	42.91	72
M.T.F.L.	34	17	0.070	5	128	2	6.12	10
S.S.I./Artisan	7	3	0.163	11	89	1.5	1.35	2
Small Business	18	8.6	0.220	15	614	11	7.42	13
R.T.O.	2	1	0.020	1	64	1	0.53	.8
Professional & Self-employed	–	–	–	–	5	.0008	0.22	.002
Others	1	.4	0.050	4	42	.7	1.22	2
Total	211	100	1473	100	5455	100	59.77	100

Staffing Pattern and Training

The staff strength during the year 1980 was as follows:

(a) Deputed Officer 5 (including Chairman)

(b) Junior Clerk/Typist 5

Due to the time constraint the bank could not arrange any training programme through the sponsor bank. But Senior Deputy Officers lent a great support in imparting job training to the directly recruited employees.

The comparative figures of staff strength for the years 1981 and 1982 are as follows:

	As on 31.12.1981	As on 31.12.1982
1. Branch Manager	11	17
2. Field Supervisor	—	10
3. Junior Clerk-cum-Cashier	19	26
4. Waterman-cum-Messenger	13	18
5. Deputed Officer	7	6
	50	77

The statutory obligation of the sponsor bank is to impart training to the directly recruit staff members of the bank. The staff members who received training from different institutions during the year 1982 are stated below:

Name of the Course	Sponsored by	No. of employee Participated
1. Rural Agricultural Project	A.R.D.C.	1
2. Inspection on the job training	United Bank of India	1

3. Inland Fishery Project	NABARD	1
4. Mixed Course Training	United Bank of India	4
5. Basic Course Training	A.R.D.C. C.L.D.B. Training Centre, Uttarpara	2

Branches

In 1980 there were two branches of Nadia Gramin Bank. In 1981 branches increased to twelve. In 1982 number of branches further increased to 17. Total rural population living in the area of operation of the bank is 23,38,848 (census of 1981). If one branch is required for every 50,000 of population then the number of branches should rise to more than 46. As it is evident from the Annual Reports of Nadia Gramin Bank, the branch expansion plan was hampered due to communication difficulty and non-availability of basic infrastructure facility, *i.e.* road communications, transport etc. Without sufficient branch expansion the very object of rural banking will remain unfulfilled.

Recovery Performance

Against the demand of Rs. 2.62 Lakhs, the recovery was of the order of Rs. 2.41 Lakhs in 1981. The recovery against the total demand was 91.98 per cent and overdue amount stood at Rs. 0.21 Lakhs. Against the demand of Rs. 11.61 Lakhs the recovery was of the order of Rs. 5.92 Lakhs in 1982. The recovery against the total demand was 51 per cent and overdue amount stood at Rs. 5.69 Lakhs.

Average Amount of Deposit and Advances Per Branch

Table NGB-5 shows average amount per branch of deposits and advances of the branches of the bank grouped according to the year of start. It is evident from the table that deposits per branch were steadily increasing as it was growing older. The rate of increase over the previous year was highest (108%) in the third year of functioning of a branch.

Table NGB-5
Average Amount of Deposit and Advances Per Branch of Nadia Gramin Bank as in 1982

Year of Start	*Average deposit per branch (Rs. 1000)*	*Average advance per branch (Rs. 1000)*
1980	788	575
1981	378	407
1982	263	193

Table NGB-6
Credit Deposit Ratios of Branches as in 1982 by Year of Start

Year of Start	*Credit Deposit Ratio*
1980	0.72
1981	1.07
1982	0.73

The rate of growth of advance in the second year of service is worked out from the available data to be 111% over the first year and in the third year 198% over the first year.

Credit-deposit ratio

On the average the credit-deposit ratio of the rate of utilization of funds of a branch improved from 0.73 to 1.07 in the second year of service but failed to 0.72 in the third year (Table NGB-6).

6. SAGAR GRAMIN BANK

The area of operation of Sagar Gramin Bank comprises the district of Twenty-four Parganas. Total population of Twenty-four Parganas is 1,07,26,751. Total rural population is 65,54,132 which comprises 61.10% of total population. Total number of main workers is 27,91,432 of which cultivators are 6,07,126, agricultural labourers are 6,10,680, household industry workers are 1,28,994 and other workers are 14,44,632 and percentages of cultivators, agricultural labourers, household industry workers and other workers are 21.75%, 21.88%, 4.62% and 51.75% respectively.[16]

Area of the district is 13,796 sq. kms.[17] Annual rainfall is 1571.6 mm. According to the statistics of 1978-79, area under rice is 612.9 thousand hectares, production is 1031.8 thousand tons and yield is 1683 kgs. per hectare. Are under wheat is 19.2 thousand hectares. Production is 45.3 thousand tons and yield is 2359 kgs. per hectare. Area under other cereals is 0.1 thousand hectares. Production is 0.1 thousand tons and yield is 1000 kgs. per hectare. Areaunder pulses is 54.4 thousand hectares. Production is 27.6 thousand tons and yield is 507 kgs. per hectare.

Average population per branch of commercial bank is 31,000.[18]

There are thirty towns in Twenty-four Parganas according to the census definition of 1981. 33 branches of Sagar Gramin Bank were started in 1981. Of these, two branches of Sagar Gramin Bank are set up in towns, remaining thirty-one branches being located in areas not specified as towns in the census of 1981.

The northern part of the district of 24-Parganas belongs to the alluvial region sharing in all its ecological characteristics. Southern part of the district is included in the coastal region with saline soil reaction. The soil types of this area are clay and clay loam. The soils here are deficient in nitrogen and phosphates but rich in potash content. In this area there is scope of growing cotton, groundnut, sunflower, sugarbeet in the Rabi season as well as kharif vegetables.

Capital and Growth

Sagar Gramin Bank was established on 24 September, 1980 with its head office at Amtala in 24-Parganas. It was sponsored by United Bank of India, Sagar Gramin Bank initiated business with a paid up share capital of Rs. 25 Lakhs. The sponsoring bank contributed 35 per cent of its paid up share capital which amounted to Rs. 8.75 Lakhs. The Government of India contributed Rs. 12.50 Lakhs or 50 per cent o the total paid up capital, the rest 15 per cent or Rs. 3.75 Lakhs came from the Government of West Bengal. The authorised capital of the bank was fixed at Rs. 1 crore. The proportions of contribution to the share-capital of the bank were fixed by statutory provision. According to its Annual Reports Sagar Gramin Bank borrowed Rs. 24.69 Lakhs from the Reserve Bank of India in 1981 and it borrowed Rs. 120.49

Lakhs from the Reserve Bank of India in 1982. The borrowing of the bank was nil in the year 1980.

The progress of the bank in various fields is given in Table SGB-1. It may be seen from the table that deposits of the bank increased considerably from Rs. 1.80 Lakhs in 1980 to Rs. 68.74 Lakhs in 1981. The increase was by 3718 per cent. In 1982 deposits further rose to Rs. 276.34 Lakhs. The increase was by 321 per cent. The advances of the bank also increased by 8059 per cent and 284 per cent respectively in 1981 and 1982. The bank suffered losses in 1980, 1981 and 1982. The loss in 1980 was due to the revenue expenditure incurred during the initial period of its incorporation, as also due to delay in its inauguration and consequent loss on house rent and others. The loss in 1981 was due to limited span of operation of less than 6 months for most of the branches and rapid branch expansion performance during the year. Loss in 1982 was mainly due to the following:

(*a*) As per directive of Reserve Bank of India and Government of India, a number of branches were opened during the year. The newly opened branches could not get adequate time to take off for advances.

(*b*) Increase in establishment cost due to enhancement of salaries of staff.

Table SGB-1

Progress of Sagar Gramin Bank during 1980-82

	1980	*1981*	*1982*
Branches	2	35	74
Deposits	1.80	68.74	276.84
(Rs. Lakhs)		(3718)	(321)
Advances	0.59	48.14	184.00

(Rs. Lakhs)		(8059)	(284)
Income	0.18	6.05	19.47
(Rs. Lakhs)		(3261)	(222)
Expenditure	0.60	12.14	46.05
(Rs. Lakhs)		(1923)	(271)
Profit & Loss	(–) 0.42	(–) 6.09	(–) 26.58
(Rs. Lakhs)			

Figures in brackets are percentage increases over the previous years.

Composition of deposits of the bank according to their categories presented in Table SGB-2 shows that Savings Bank deposits were persistently predominant during all the three years constituting 46 per cent, 76 per cent and 68 per cent respectively in the years 1980, 1981 and 1982. Next in importance was fixed deposit which increased from 13 per cent in 1981 to 27 per cent in 1982. So it is clear that the bank was able to mobilize surpluses of the rural households. The performance in the sphere of deposit mobilization was definitely a big achievement. The task of deposit mobilization had to proceed in the face of manpower problem, infrastructural inadequacy and other related constraints. With the introduction of Swalpa Sanchay Scheme (Small Savings Scheme), intensive efforts were made to popularise the small savings habit among the villagers. According to the Annual Report of the Bank for the year 1980 the average amount of deposit per account was Rs. 411 at the end of 1980. It was found on analysis, that about 96 per cent depositors were from people of smaller means comprising farmers, artisans and small retailers. The average amount of deposit per account in 1981 was Rs. 360 only and it was Rs. 424 in 1982.

Loaning Operations

The items of activities for which the bank provided credit in 1981 and 1982 were agriculture, small scale industries, Road/water transport operators, retail and small business, business of professional and self-employed persons as shown in Table SGB-3. The table indicates that agriculture had the largest share of the credit facilities which was 55 per cent of the total in 1981 and 53 per cent in 1982. Retail and small business captured the next place, receiving around 25 per cent of the total loans in 1981 and 28 per cent in 1982. The small-scale industries also rose to prominance by commanding about 13 per cent of the loans in 1982.

Table SGB-2
Composition of Deposits by Category

Category	*1980 Amount (Rs. Lakhs)*	*1981 Amount (Rs. Lakhs)*	*1982 Amount (Rs. Lakhs)*
Fixed Deposit	0.80 (45)	9.30 (13)	74.80 (27)
Savings Bank Deposits	0.83 (46)	52.41 (76)	186.79 (68)
Current Account	0.17 (9)	7.32 (11)	15.26 (6)
Total	1.80 (100)	69.03 (100)	276.85 (100)

(Figures in brackets are percentages to total).

The average amount of loan per account was only Rs. 632 in 1980, Rs. 1274 in 1981 and Rs. 1129 in 1982.

Table SGB-3
Disbursement of Loans at Sagar Gramin Bank

Items	*Amount of Loans Disbursed*			
	1981		*1982*	
	Rs. Lakhs	*%*	*Rs. Lakhs*	*%*
Agriculture (short-term & medium term): share croppers,marginal farmers & small farmers.	25.54	55.4	91.13	53
S.S.I.	4.48	9.7	21.40	12.7
Road/Water Transport Operators	4.47	9.7	10.81	6
Retail and Small Business	11.38	24.68	48.26	27.5
Professional & Self-employed persons	0.23	.52	3.22	.20
Others	Nil	–	9.74	.60
Total	46.10	100	184.56	100

Recovery of Loans

Recovery of loans was 92 per cent in 1981 and 74 per cent in 1982. So it can be said that overall recovery performance is better.

Staffing Pattern and Training

At the end of 1982 the staff of the bank consisted of 69 Officers, 50 Field Supervisors, 6 Senior Clerk-cum-Cashiers, 63 Junior Clerk-cum-Cashiers. During 1982 the bank availed itself of the opportunity of getting the personnel trained in United Bank of India Staff Training College, as also in College of Agricultural Banking, Pune in different courses. While the courses conducted at UBI Staff Training College were mixed courses of 3 days' to

2 weeks' duration, the courses at CAB, Pune were of 4 weeks duration on Integrated Rural Development Programme, Rural Financing and Agro-based Industries. Besides a short course for field supervisors of 3 days duration on rural financing was conducted by the bank in collaboration with UBISTC. 3 days' training was also organised by Sagar Gramin Bank Training Centre at Jyangra. Training was also conducted by NABARD and Agricultural Refinance Development Corporation.

Branches

In 1980 there were 2 branches. In 1982 the number rose to 35. And in 1982 there were 74 branches within one year. This implied that number of branches increased by more than 111 per cent in one year. Total rural population living in the area of operation of the bank is 65,54,132 (census of 1981). If one branch is required for every 50,000 of population then the number of branches should rise to 131. There is no doubt that the success of rural banking will depend to a greater extent on branch expansion which in turn depends on availability of trained personnel having rural orientation and aptitude, infrastructural facilities and training programme for staff of Rural Banks at all levels.

Average Amount of Deposit and Advances Per Branch

Table SGB-4 shows the average amount per branch of deposits and advances of the branches of the bank grouped according to the year of their start. Both the average amount of deposits and advances per branch greatly increased in the second and third year of the functioning of the branch.

Table SGB-4
Average Amount of Deposit and Advances Per Branch of Sagar Gramin Bank as in 1982

Year of Start	*Average deposit per branch (Rs. 1000)*	*Average advance per branch (Rs. 1000)*
1980	2038	1533
1981	512	408
1982	174	147

Table SGB-5
Credit Deposit Ratio for Branches as in 1982 by Year of Start

Year of Start	*Credit Deposit Ratio*
1980	0.75
1981	0.79
1982	0.84

On the average the second year and the third year of a branch witnessed rise in deposits by 200 per cent and 300 per cent respectively. Similarly the second and third year of a branch on the average recorded a rise in advances by 178 per cent and 275 per cent respectively. Thus the progress of an average branch continued uninterrupted during the period under review.

Table SGB-5 shows that credit-deposit-ratio which is index of utilization of the resources of a bank was falling for an average branch during the period in question.

7. BARDHAMAN GRAMIN BANK

Area of operation of Bardhaman Gramin Bank consists of two districts namely, Burdwan and Hooghly. Total population of Burdwan district is 48,08,886. Total rural population is 33,83,227 comprising 70.38% of total population. Total main workers are 13,46,772 in number of which cultivators are 3,13,535, agricultural labourers are 4,08,296, household industry workers are 51,111 and other workers are 5,73,830 and percentages of cultivators, agricultural labourers, household industry workers, and other workers to total workers are 23.28%, 30.32%, 3.80% and 42.60% respectively.[19]

Area of the district is 7028 sq. kms.[20] Annual rainfall is 1358.0 mm. According to 1978-79 statistics area of rice cultivation is 448.3 thousand hectares, production of rice is 1009.4 thousand tonnes. Yield is 2252 kgs. per hectare. Area under wheat is 26.4 thousand hectares. Production of wheat is 51.6 thousand tonnes. Yield is 1956 kgs. per hectare. Area under other cereals is 1.5 thousand hectares. Production of other cereals is 0.7 thousand tonnes. Yield is 467 kgs. per hectare. Area under pulses is 10.6 thousand tonnes. Yield is 505 kgs. per hectare.

Average population per branch of commercial bank is 22,000.[21]

There are fifty-three towns in Burdwan district according to the census definition of 1981. Eleven branches were set up in Burdwan upto 1981 of which one town has a branch of Bardhaman Gramin Bank. Remaining branches were set up in 1981 in areas not specified as towns in census of 1981. Seven branches were set up in Hooghly district by 1981 and all these branches were placed in areas not specified as towns in the census of 1981.

Total population of Hooghly district is 35,49,817. Total rural population is 25,01,065 comprising 70.46% of total population. Total main workers are 10,13,053 in number of whom cultivators are 2,44,011, agricultural labourers are 2,81,323, household industry workers are 40,572 and other workers are 4,47,147 and percentages of cultivators, agricultural labourers, household industry workers and other workers to total workers are 24.09, 27.77, 4.00 and 44.14 respectively.

Area of the district is 3145 sq. kms.[2] Annual rainfall is 1582.2 mm. In 1978-79 area of rice cultivation is 256.1 thousand hectares. Production of rice is 846.7 thousand tonnes. Yield is 1354 kgs. per hectare. Area under wheat is 17.2 thousand hectares. Production of wheat is 34.0 thousand tonnes. Yield is 1975 kgs. per hectare. Area under pulses is 8.8 thousand hectares. Production of pulses is 3.4 thousand tonnes. Yield is 386 kgs. per hectare.

Average population per branch of commercial bank is 23,000.

Both the districts of Burdwan and Hooghly are in the alluvial region. Soil-types of the area are loam, clay loam, sandy loam, sandy clay loam. Part of the district of Burdwan (Asansol subdivision) is, however, laterite with sandy clay loam and clay loam with concretion. There is scope of extension of area under wheat, pulses and oilseeds in this region with suitable irrigation.

Capital and Growth

Bardhaman Gramin Bank was established on 25th

November, 1980 under the sponsorship of United Commercial Bank with its head office at Burdwan. Bardhaman Gramin Bank started business with a paid up share capital of Rs. 25 Lakhs. The sponsoring bank contributed 35 per cent of its paid up share capital which amounted to Rs. 8.75 Lakhs. The Government of India contributed Rs. 12.50 Lakhs or 50 per cent of the total paid up capital, the remaining 15 per cent or Rs. 3.75 Lakhs came from Government of West Bengal. The authorised capital of the bank was fixed at Rs. 1 crore. The proportions of participation in the share-capital of the bank were fixed by statutory provision. According to the Annual Report of the Bank it borrowed Rs. 9.50 Lakhs from NABARD and Rs. 25 Lakhs from United Commercial Bank in 1982. Borrowing of the bank was nil in 1980 and 1981.

The progress of the bank in various respects is given in Table BGB-1. It may be seen from the table that deposits increased considerably from Rs. 0.06 Lakhs in 1980 to Rs. 10.81 Lakhs in 1981. The increase was by 17916 per cent. In 1982 deposit further increased to Rs. 68.69 Lakhs. The increase was 535 per cent. The advances of the bank increased by 33455 per cent in 1982.

Table BGB-1

Progress of Bardhaman Gramin Bank during 1980-82

	1980	*1981*	*1982*
Branches	1	18	30
Deposits	0.06	10.81	68.69
(Rs. Lakhs)		(17916)	(535)
Advances	Nil	0.09	30.20
(Rs. Lakhs)			(33455)
Income	Nil	3.74	5.38
(Rs. Lakhs)			(44)

Expenditure (Rs. Lakhs)	0.03	3.96 (13100)	15.64 (295)
Profit & Loss (Rs. Lakhs)	(-) 0.03	(-) 0.22	(-) 10.01

Figures in brackets are percentage increases over the previous years.

The bank suffered losses in 1980, 1981 and 1982. Losses were mainly due to the following factors:

(a) As per directive of Reserve Bank of India and Government of India, a number of branches were opened during the year. The newly opened branches could not get sufficient time to prepare for making judicious advances, and

(b) Establishment cost increased for the enhancement of salaries of staff.

Table BGB-2

Composition of Deposits by Category

Category	*1980 Amount (Rs. Lakhs)*	*1981 Amount (Rs. Lakhs)*	*1982 Amount (Rs. Lakhs)*
Fixed and Time Deposits	Nil	0.70 (7)	12.93 (19)
Savings Bank Deposits	0.06 (100)	9.32 (86)	53.65 (78)
Current Account	Nil	0.79 (7)	2.03 (3)
Total	0.06 (100)	10.81 (100)	68.61 (100)

(Figures in brackets are percentages to total)

Composition of deposits of the bank according to their categories as shown in Table BGB-2 shows that Savings Bank deposits were predominant during all the three years constituting 100 per cent, 86 per cent and

78 per cent respectively in the years 1980, 1981 and 1982. Next in importance was fixed deposit which increased from 7 per cent in 1981 to 19 per cent in 1982.

Loaning Operations

The items of activities for which the bank disbursed credit in 1982 were agriculture, small business, road transport, small-scale industries, artisans and activities of self-employed persons as shown in Table BGB-3. The table shows that the major part of the credit facilities of the bank were allocated to agriculture and small business persons covering around 58.03 per cent and 27.75 per cent respectively in 1982. Most of the credit available for agriculture was short-term loans. Loaning operation of the bank was insignificant in the initial years.

Table BGB-3
Disbursement of Loans at Bardhaman Gramin Bank

Items	*Amount of Loans Disbursed*			
	1981		*1982*	
	Rs. Lakhs	*%*	*Rs. Lakhs*	*%*
Agriculture (short-term & medium term): share croppers, marginal farmers & small farmers.	Nil	–	17.52	58.03
Small Business	0.09	100	8.38	27.75
S.S.I. & Artisans	Nil	–	0.70	2.31
Road Transport Operators	Nil	–	1.30	4.30
Self-employed persons	Nil	–	1.39	4.60
Advance against deposit & others	Nil	–	0.91	3.01
Total	0.09	100	30.20	100

Staffing Pattern and Training

At the end of 1982 the staff of the bank consisted of 27 Officers, 28 Field Supervisors, 21 Junior Clerk-cum-Cashiers, 2 Junior Clerk-cum-Typists, 25 Messenger-cum-Sweepers, 1 Deputy Officer (excluding the Chairman). Few staff undertook training in agriculture at Indian Agricultural Research Institute and some of them had undertaken cooperative training.

Branches

There was only one branch in 1980. In 1981 number of branches increased to 18 within one year. In 1982, there were 30 branches. Total rural population living in the area of operation of the bank is 56,84,292 (census of 1981). If one branch is required for every 50,000 of population then the number of branches should rise to 118.

Table BGB-4
Average Amount of Deposit and Advances Per Branch of Bardhaman Gramin Bank as in 1982

Year of Start	*Average deposit per branch (Rs. 1000)*	*Average advance per branch (Rs. 1000)*
1981	326	359
1982	80	104

Average Amount of Deposit and Advances Per Branch

Table BGB-4 shows the average amount per branch of deposits and advances of the branches of the bank grouped according to the year of their start. It is found from the table that a branch one year old could mobilize Rs. 3.26 Lakhs as deposits and could advance Rs. 3.59

Lakhs as loans. The rise in per branch deposit per year seems to be about 300 per cent. The advances rose per branch at the rate of 245 per cent a year. However, these rates worked out from one year's functioning of a branch can be taken only with caution. It must need to be revised with the passage of time.

Credit-deposit Ratio

It may be seen from Table BGB-5 that credit-deposit ratio of a branch on the average declined a little from 1.3 to 1.10 within a year of its functioning.

Table BGB-5

Credit Deposit Ratios of Branches as in 1982 by Year of Start

Year of Start	*Credit Deposit Ratio*
1981	1.10
1982	1.03

On the whole it appears that the progress of the Bardhaman Gramin Bank was hindered by the competition of commercial banks' density of which in its area of operation was quite high.

At the end of the present chapter it may be noted that further consideration is given to credit-deposit ratios of different RRBs in Chapter 7 on comparative assessment of the Regional Rural Banks.

REFERENCES

1. Census of India 1981, Series 23, West Bengal.
2. Govt. of West Bengal, Statistical Handbook, 1979.
3. Govt. of West Bengal, Economic Review, 1980-81.

4. Census of India, 1981, Series 23, West Bengal.
5. Govt. of West Bengal, Statistical Handbook, 1979.
6. Govt. of West Bengal, Economic Review, 1980-81.
7. Census of India 1981, Series 23 West Bengal.
8. Govt. of West Bengal, Statistical Handbook 1979.
9. Govt. of West Bengal, Economic Review 1980-81.
10. Census of India, 1981, Series 23 West Bengal.
11. Govt. of West Bengal, Statistical Handbook, 1979.
12. Govt. of West Bengal, Economic Review, 1980-81.
13. Census of India 1981, Series 23 West Bengal.
14. Govt. of West Bengal, Statistical Handbook, 1979.
15. Govt. of West Bengal, Economic Review, 1980-81.
16. Census of India 1981, Series 23 West Bengal.
17. Govt. of West Bengal, Statistical Handbook, 1979.
18. Govt. of West Bengal, Economic Review, 1980-81.
19. Census of India 1981, Series 23 West Bengal.
20. Govt. of West Bengal, Statistical Handbook, 1979.
21. Govt. of West Bengal, Economic Review, 1980-81.

6

Rates of Interest on Deposits, Borrowings and Lending and Mode of Loaning Operations

Deposits and borrowings of the Regional Rural Banks are the major components of working capital of the Regional Rural Banks.

The deposits are composed mainly of current deposits, Savings Bank Deposits and Fixed Deposits. It has been seen in Chapter 5 that Savings Bank Deposits were the largest components of savings of the RRB and grew at higher rates than the other types of deposits.

The borrowings of the RRBs were mostly from the Reserve Bank of India. The other sources of borrowings were the sponsoring banks, the Agricultural Refinance and Development Corporation and Industrial Development Bank of India.

1. The Fixed Deposits of the RRBs were of different

terms, such as from 15 to 45 days, 46 to 90 days, 91 days to 6 months, 6 months to 9 months, 9 to 12 months, 1 year to 3 years, 3 years to 5 years and above 5 years, bearing 3%, 3.5%, 4.5%, 5%, 5.5%, 6%, 6.5% - 7.5%, 8% - 9%, 9% - 10% respectively during 1978-80. In 1981 the rates of interest were raised to 8% and 9% respectively for the deposits of terms 1-2 years and 2-3 years. These categories of terms were created by splitting the terms 1-3 years and 2 to 3 years. In 1981 the term above 5 years bearing 10% rate of interest was revised to be 3 years and above. Thus there was liberalization both in respect of term and the rate of interest.

In general, the Fixed Deposits were bearing rates of interest which were 0.50% higher than the rates of commercial banks. While the rate of interest for Savings Bank Deposits was 5% per annum for the commercial banks, the RRBs continued to pay 5.5% on their Savings Bank Deposits throughout the period 1978-1981. While the rates of interest on Savings Banks Deposits were the same for District Central Cooperative Banks, they paid slightly lower rates of interest for Fixed Deposits. The District Central Cooperative Banks unlike RRBs had some special categories of deposits, *e.g.*, Staff security fund, Risk fund of societies and Reserve fund of societies bearing 11%, 10½% and 10½% respectively.

It cannot, however, be said that the remarkable growth of Savings Bank deposits at the RRBs were due to the higher rates of interest they offered. Perhaps the progress was more due to the close proximity of the RRBs to the villagers and the growth of banking habit among them. Even if an equal rate of interest were offered by the commercial banks it is doubtful whether they would have been able to dievrt those funds away from the RRBs. The higher rates of interest on Fixed Deposits failed to serve as a stimulus to their growth. This shows that rural savings lacked sensitivity to the rate of interest and were more under the pressure of liquidity preference. In fact, the RRBs offered opportunity to the surplus-making villagers to hold their savings in semi-liquid condition which, in their turn, met part of the short-term credit-needs of the borrowing villagers. Thus an institutional linkage between rural savings and rural investments was at least partially developed through the Savings Bank Accounts of the RRBs.

The RRBs were paying 7.5% rate of interest on their normal borrowings from the Reserve Bank of India, 8.5% and 7.5% on similar loans from the sponsoring banks and ARDC/NABARD respectively. Schematic loans from the Reserve Bank of India and ARDC/NABARD were bearing 6.5% rate of interest. The District Central Cooperative Banks had the facility of obtaining short-term and mid-term agricultural loans at the rate of 6.75% and Handloom borrowing at 6.50% from the State Cooperative Bank. Rates of interest on the short-term agricultural loans of RRBs upto Rs. 2500 and above Rs. 2500 were 11% and 13% respectively during 1979. Term loans for land development and other diversified purposes had to bear 9.5% rate of interest during 1979. Indirect loans disbursed through primary agricultural credit societies and farmers service societies etc. had to bear 8% in the case of small farmers and 9% in the case of other farmers. Rates of interest on short-term loans for small business, rural artisans, self-employed persons, transport operators etc. in the non-agricultural sector upto Rs. 2500 and above Rs. 2500 were 11% and 13% respectively. For mid-term loans the rate was 10.5%. Rates of interest charged by cooperatives on short and mid-term loans were 11% and 12% respectively.

In 1980 rates of interest on short-term lendings (crop loan) of RRBs upto Rs. 2500 and above Rs. 2500 were raised to 11.5% and 14% respectively. Rates of interest on term loans for minor irrigations, land development and other diversified purposes were raised to 10%. Rates of interest for indirect loans and most of the other categories of loans were raised 0.5%. Rate of interest on loans for small business, rural artisans etc. in the non-agricultural sector was raised to 14%. Correspondingly, rates of interest to be charged by societies to the ultimate borrowers of indirect loans were raised to rates varying from 10.25% to 14%, depending upon the type of loan.

In 1981 the rates of interest on loans for small farmers (short, medium and long term) upto Rs. 5000 were raised to 12.50%. Provisions of agricultural loans from Rs. 5000 to Rs. 25,000 bearing 15% rate of interest and above Rs. 25,000 bearing 17.50% were introduced. Differential rate of interest to the extent of as low as 4% for special categories of loans was also a new feature. Some unspecified priority sector loans were also provided for, bearing as high as 19.50% rate of interest. Rates of interest on loans for minor irrigation and land development, going to small farmers were raised to 10.25%, other farmers paying 12.50%.

On non-agricultural sector loans, too, rates of interest underwent more or less similar rise.

It seems that the lending rates of interest charged by the RRBs are not appreciably lower than those of the commercial banks which are usually 12.5% for short-term agricultural loans upto Rs. 5000 on this score. Therefore RRBs may not be of special benefit to the rural area except that they make more credit available to the weaker sections of the rural community. However, the RRB rates are very much lower than those charged by the private money lenders. Lending rates of the Central Cooperative Banks for short-term and mid-term agricultural loans were 10% and 11% respectively. These were lower than the similar RRB loans.

If, from the foregoing data, the rate of interest on deposits and borrowings of the RRBs is estimated at 8% per annum and the lending rate affecting major portion of the loans (crop loans) is estimated at 12% per annum, there should accrue a net interest-earning from loaning operations of the RRBs to the extent of 4% per annum. Apparently, this margin should prove big enough to enable the RRBs to earn profit.

If the profit margin could be increased further, then even smaller scale of business would have enabled the RRBs to earn profit. Profit margin can be increased in two ways, either by increasing lending rate or by availability of borrowing at lower rates of interest. But if the lending rates are raised then the very objective of RRBs to provide cheap credit for the rural sector is defeated. Again if the borrowing rates are lowered, that will mean a sacrifice on the part of the public and discourage deposits of the public sector banks. The ultimate consequence will be a diminution in their capacity to lend funds to the RRBs.

2. The scale of financing fixed by the RRBs for agriculture is based on details of cost of cultivation in accordance with the recommendation of the Government of West Bengal. In sanctioning credit it is considered that the amount of credit meets the entire cost for seed, manure, fertilizer, pesticides, irrigation and 50% of labour input.

The scale of finance for different crops per hectare basis are presented in Table 6.1.

From Table 6.1 it is apparent that the scale of finance is highest (Rs. 10625) in the case of potato and lowest for pulses, depending upon cost of cultivation. Rate of every input is highest for potato, seed covering 56% of the total cost. Next to potato is Boro (HYV summer rice) which demands a scale of finance to the extent of Rs. 4355 per hectare. Rate of irrigation input per hectare is also subject to a great deal of variation according to requirement of water.

Loan is offered to the borrowers partly in cash and partly in the form of direct payment by the banks to the suppliers on behalf of the borrowers. Cash portion of the loans is to cover manure and labour only. If irrigation is supplied by approved sources, payments are made directly by the banks to them. Otherwise case part of credit would include cost of irrigation, too.

The short-term crop loan is treated as demand loan which is repayable within 18 months. In other cases of short-term loan provided as working capital it is repayable within 3 years. It is always treated as production loan or working capital. No direct asset is created out of short-term loan.

In case of investment loan some sort of asset is created out of loan. The term of repayment is mid-term or long-term.

In case of short-term crop loan the method of assessment of requirement is cost of production per unit of land. In case of short-term non-agricultural loan the amount is fixed according to the extent of the working capital required.

Regarding mid-term loan the method of assessment

Table 6.1

Scale of Finance for Different Crops Per Hectare

S. No.	*Crop*	*Seed*	*Manure*	*Fertilizer*	*Pesticides*	*Irrigation*	*Labour*	*Total*	*Scale of Finance/acre*
1	*2*	*3*	*4*	*5*	*6*	*7*	*8*	*9*	*10*
1.	Rice (Traditional)	150/-	200/-	300/- (30:15:15)	125/-	150/- (15")	1000/-	1925/-	770/-
2.	Rice (HYV) Kharif	150/-	200/-	500/- (50:25:25)	250/-	300/- (30")	1250/-	2650/-	1060/-
3.	Rice (HYV) Boro	180/-	250/-	800/- (80:20:20)	425/-	1200/- (120")	1500/-	4355/-	1740/-
4.	Jute	50/-	250/-	400/- (40:20:20)	200/-	200/- (20")	1500/-	2600/-	1040/-
5.	Maize	75/-	250/-	400/- (40:20:20)	100/-	450/- (45")	750/-	2025/-	810/-
6.	Wheat	400/-	250/-	600/- (60:30:30)	100/-	300/- (30")	1000/-	2650/-	1060/-
7.	Mustard	50/-	250/-	300/- (30:15:15)	100/-	100/- (10")	750/-	1560/-	620/-
8.	Pulses	200/-	250/-	200/- (10:30:00)	50/-	200/- (20")	400/-	1250/-	550/-
9.	Potato	6000/-	500/-	1750/- (150:100:100)	250/-	500/- (50")	1625/-	10625/-	4250/-
10.	Vegetables	150/-	250/-	1200/- (120:60:60)	150/-	450/- (45")	1000/-	3200/-	1280/-

Source: United Commercial Bank, West Bengal Division III.

of requirement is the cost to acquire the asset including capitalised working cost.

In case of short-term crop loan disbursement of loans depends upon the components of cost of production.

1. Cash component (30% to 70%)
2. Kind component (30% to 70%) by delivery order generally through cooperatives.
3. In case of agricultural term loan (M.T.) non-living equipment as pumpset, thresher, sprayer etc. as per quotation through delivery order.

In case of draught animals etc. Bank arranges the purchase on behalf of the loanee. Regarding short-term agricultural loan supervision is not needed generally. In case of M.T. loan utilization of the loan is checked by regular visit.

The time of repayment of S.T. crop loan depends from sowing to harvesting and marketing of the crop. In case of M.T. loan, the loan should be repaid by instalment (half-yearly or annually). The time period of repayment of M.T. agricultural loan depends upon the economic life time of the assets acquired out of loan and the extent of income derived out of the utilization of the assets. In case of M.T. (non-agricultural) loan the recovery period depends upon the economy life time of the assets acquired out of loan (monthly or quarterly).

Recovery schedule (monthly, quarterly or annually, whatever it may be) depends upon time lag of the production process—from raw materials to marketing *i.e.* from cash to cash according to banking term.

3. Different types of security (collateral) are required by the RRBs for loans of different categories.

For crop loans upto Rs. 1000, Rs. 1000-5000 and

above Rs. 5000 securities to be furnished are: (1) D.P. Note and Letter of Waiver, (2) D.P. Note, Letter of Waiver and Execution of Loan Agreement, and (3) D.P. Note, Letter of Waiver, Execution of Loan Agreement, Mortgage of Land or a third party guarantee respectively.

In respect of term loans upto Rs. 5000 D.P. Note, Letter of Waiver and Execution of Loan Agreement are demanded by way of security. For term loans over Rs. 5000 D.P. Note, Letter of Waiver, Loan Agreement, Mortgage of Land or a third party guarantee are the requirements.

D.P. Note, Letter of Waier, Loan Agreement and Creation of Mortgage of Land are required for loans of Rs. 1000 and above whicn are not meant for creating movable assets. Such loans, for example, include those for land development, construction of sheds, house of dairy, poultry, piggery etc, construction of godown/grain sheds, grain gola/threshing floors, farm sheds etc.

The taking of mortgage of land as security, wherever it is provided for, has to be left to the discretion of the Chairman. As per West Bengal Agricultural Credit Operation Act 1973, a simple declaration (Nidarsa) creating a change on the land offered as security will suffice in case of agricultural loans. In such cases registered mortgage of land will not be necessary. Thus, it may be seen that for loans there is little stringency regarding collateral. Material collateral is not required in their cases. The offer of land mortgage for loans of bigger amounts involves a very simple procedure such as declaration.

On the whole, it may be noted that the loans are made available to the rural borrowers on easy terms in regard to amount, rates of interest, collateral and period of repayment so that the dispensation of credit suits their requirements and facilitates the utilization of credit.*

* Sources of data on rates of interest, collateral etc. Mayurakshi Gramin Bank, Birbhum, United Bank of India, Bolpur, Birbhum, and Birbhum District Central Cooperative Bank Private Ltd. Suri, Birbhum.

7

A Comparative Assessment of the Regional Rural Banks

A comparative assessment of the Regional Rural Banks surveyed earlier (Chapter 5) is attempted in the present chapter.

Criteria used in this study are the extent of branch expansion, the extent of profit or loss, the growth of deposits and advances per branch and credit-deposit ratio.

Since the Regional Rural Banks function through branch offices, remote interior of the rural areas can be brought under their purview only if a network of branches is developed extensively. Hence is the importance of branch expansion as a yardstick.

Profit is a good indicator of efficiency. But high profit may be accompanied by a small volume of business. In that case efficiency may not be considered high in spite of high profit. Regional Rural Banks are expected to be agencies for the mobilization of rural savings which are likely to rise with the progress of agricultural technology. If local savings are mobilized and channelled through branches of the Regional Rural Banks to small enterprises of the local areas, pressure upon national finance capital is relieved to a considerable extent. Growth of deposits is, therefore, a good yardstick for assessing the performance of a Regional Rural Bank so also the growth of advances which contribute to the alleviation of scarcity of rural credit.

Another indicator of efficiency is credit-deposit ratio which reflects the intensity of utilization of funds. Recovery of loans, to, is an indicator of the efficiency of performance because recovery of loans signifies profitability of investment.

Average number of branches, average amounts of profit or loss and average amounts of deposits and advances during the last three years are taken into account to eliminate chance variation in the magnitudes to some extent.

In the case of branches latest numbers of branches are also given to indicate the rate of expansion over the average of the last three years (Table 7.1). A place has also been given to the comparison of the number of agricultural workers coming under the purview of the area of operation of a RRB with the total volume of its business operation. This would indicate the intansity of business operation of a RRB.

This chapter also makes a special attempt to probe deeply the issue of profit or loss experienced by the RRBs.

The Regional Rural Banks named after Nadia, Sagar and Bardhaman are comparatively of recent origin. Hence the rate of branch expansion was higher in their cases. However, the latest number of branches (74) in the case of Sagar Regional Rural Bank and its 100% expansion of branches over the average of the last three years are rather remarkable. Among the older Regional Rural Banks Gour, Mayurakshi and Uttarbanga experienced branch expansion at rates varying from 33% to 62%. Mallabhum, however, had little progress in this regard (9% only). Because of the large size of its area of operation the excess number of its branches is not significant.

Table 7.1
Average Number of Branches of the Regional Rural Banks during the Last Three Years

Name of Regional Rural Banks	*Average number of branches during the last three years*	*Latest number of branches*
Mayurakshi	37	50 (135)
Gaur	42	56 (133)
Uttarbanga	35	57 (162)
Mallabhum	63	69 (109)
Nadia	10	17 (170)
Sagar	37	74 (200)
Bardhaman	16	30 (188)

(Figures in brackets are percentages on the average numbers).

Turning to the question of profit or losses, it may be seen from Table 7.2 that barring Gaur and Mallabhum all the other Regional Rural Banks suffered losses, reflecting a low level of efficiency in management of business. We also consider in this connection expenditures of the RRBs (Average of last three years) in breakdowns of establishment and interest cost.

Table 7.2
Average Profit (+) or Loss (–) of the Regional Rural Banks during the Last Three Years

Name of Regional Rural Banks	*Profit (+) or Loss (–) (Rs. Lakhs)*
Mayurakshi	– 7.91
Gaur	+ 1.51
Uttarbanga	– 7.16
Mallabhum	+ 1.84
Nadia	– 1.48
Sagar	– 11.03
Bardhaman	– 3.42

Table 7.3 shows that for all the RRBs barring Gaur Gramin Bank and Mallabhum Gramin Bank the percentage shares of salaries, allowances and other establishment costs in total expenditures are very much higher than those of interest-cost which reflects the volume of loaning business.

Thus, for Mayurakshi Gramin Bank, Uttarbanga Kshetriya Gramin Bank, Nadia Gramin Bank, Sagar Gramin Bank and Bardhaman Gramin Bank respectively the percentage shares of establishment costs in total costs were higher than those of interest costs by 29, 44, 68, 60 and 74 respectively. These explain their losses to a greater extent. It is evident that the RRBs suffering losses were not able to utilize their establishments adequately in maintaining larger volume of investments. In the case of Gaur Gramin Bank enjoying profit the percentage share of establishment cost was lower than that of interest cost by 16. For Mallabhum Gramin Bank which was also making profit the percentage share of establishment cost was only slightly higher than that of interest cost. Thus, the volume of loaning business must be large enough to ensure fuller utilization of the establishment.

Table 7.3

Average Salaries and Allowances of the Employees and Interest Paid on Deposits and Borrowings of the Rural Banks Per Annum During the Last Three Years

Name of the Bank	*Items*	*Amount (Rs. Lakhs)*
Mayurakshi Gramin Bank	Salaries, allowances and other establishment costs	16.81 (64.67)
	Interest	9.18 (35.32)
	Total Expenditure	25.99
Gaur Gramin Bank	Salaries allowances and other establishment costs	22.01 (41.65)
	Interest	30.84 (58.35)
	Total Expenditure	52.85
Uttarbanga Kshetriya Gramin Bank	Salaries allowances and other establishment costs	12.73 (72.33)
	Interest	4.87 (27.67)
	Total Expenditure	17.60
Mallabhum Gramin Bank	Salaries, allowances and other establishment costs	27.72 (50.44)
	Interest	27.24 (49.56)
	Total Expenditure	54.96
Nadia Gramin Bank	Salaries, allowances and other establishment costs	5.56 (84.24)
	Interest	1.04 (15.75)
	Total Expenditure	6.60

Sagar Gramin Bank	Salaries, allowances and other establishment costs	15.61 (79.68)
	Interest	3.98 (20.31)
	Total Expenditure	19.59
Bardhaman Gramin Bank	Salaries, allowances and other establishment costs	5.68 (86.85)
	Interest	0.86 (13.14)
	Total Expenditure	6.54

(Figures in brackets are percentages to total expenditure)

Table 7.4 presents figures of average deposits, borrowings and advances of the Regional Rural Banks for the last three years and credit-deposit ratio worked out from these figures. Credit-deposit ratio in the case of Mallabhum Regional Rural Bank is rather low (0.65) compared to those of the other older banks, such as, Mayurakshi, Gaur and Uttarbanga. Though Mallabhum meets the criterion of profitable business it fails to stand the test of high credit-deposit-ratio as an yardstick of business efficiency. Credit-deposit-ratio is particularly low (0.38 only) in the case of Bardhaman showing a poor character of its business.

Table 7.4

Average Deposits, Borrowings, Advances and Credit-Deposit Ratio of the Regional Rural Banks during the Last Three Years

Name of Regional Rural Bank	*Average Deposit (Rs. Lakhs)*	*Average Borrowings (Rs. Lakhs)*	*Average Advances (Rs. Lakhs)*	*Credit-Deposit Ratio Col.4/Col.2*
Mayurakshi	174.90	71.15	179.25	1.02
Gaur	287.23	307.56	477.46	1.66
Uttarbanga	270.94	77.04	344.34	1.27
Mallabhum	532.14	109.11	346.71	0.65
Nadia	29.35	6.43	26.97	0.92
Sagar	115.79	48.39	77.58	0.67
Bardhaman	26.52	11.50	10.09	0.38

Gaur scores highest record of efficiency both by the standard of profitable business and high credit-deposit-ratio which is 1.66 in its case.

It seems that high credit-deposit ratio of Gaur Gramin Bank has been influenced by borrowings which were immensely greater than those of other RRBs. Unfortunately, though the borrowings of Mallabhum Gramin Bank were quite high (next to Gaur), its credit-deposit ratio is low. This seems to be due to comparatively smaller advances. In the case of Uttarbanga credit-deposit ratio is higher because of higher scale of advances, though its borrowings were lower than those of Mallabhum. Other RRBs like Sagar and Bardhaman which came later could not have enough opportunity to raise their loaning business. However, the performance of Nadia is better than that of the other new RRBs in respect of advances. On the whole credit-deposit ratio depends much upon managerial efficiency in extending credit.

Out of the 7 Regional Rural Banks under the present study, Gaur, Uttarbanga and Mallabhum reported recovery of loans to the extent of 53%*, 68% and 45% respectively in 1981 (see Chapter 5).

However, apart from lack of data on recovery of loans for other Regional Rural Banks, the recovery figures quoted above are not related to the age of the debts and hence fail to indicate the extent of overdue loans. It seems that overdue loans are in general a problem for the Regional Rural Banks and these seem to be due to poor repayment capacity of the borrowers, poor supervision of the utilization of credit and poor arrangement for the collection of repayment.

As regards staffing pattern all the Regional Rural

Figure 1·1

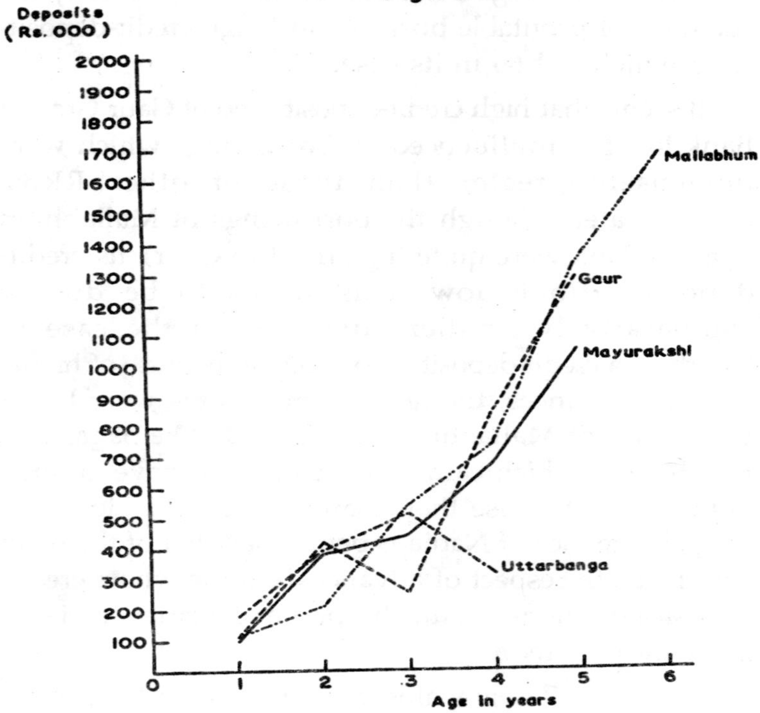

Average Deposit (Rs. 000) per Branch of a RRB by Age.

Banks are characterised by the absence of technical personnel who would conduct feasibility studies on the basis of which projects for profitable investment could be drawn up. Need for such specialised service for making loaning operations fruitful cannot be neglected.

Figures 1.1 and 1.2 indicate the growth of deposits per branch and figures 2.1 and 2.2 indicate the growth of advances per branch. Figures 1.1 and 2.1 represent the older banks, 1.2 and 2.2 representing the recent ones. These figures show the degree of progress of a branch on the average in respect of deposits and advances as distinguished from the overall progress of the RRB's on

Figure 1·2

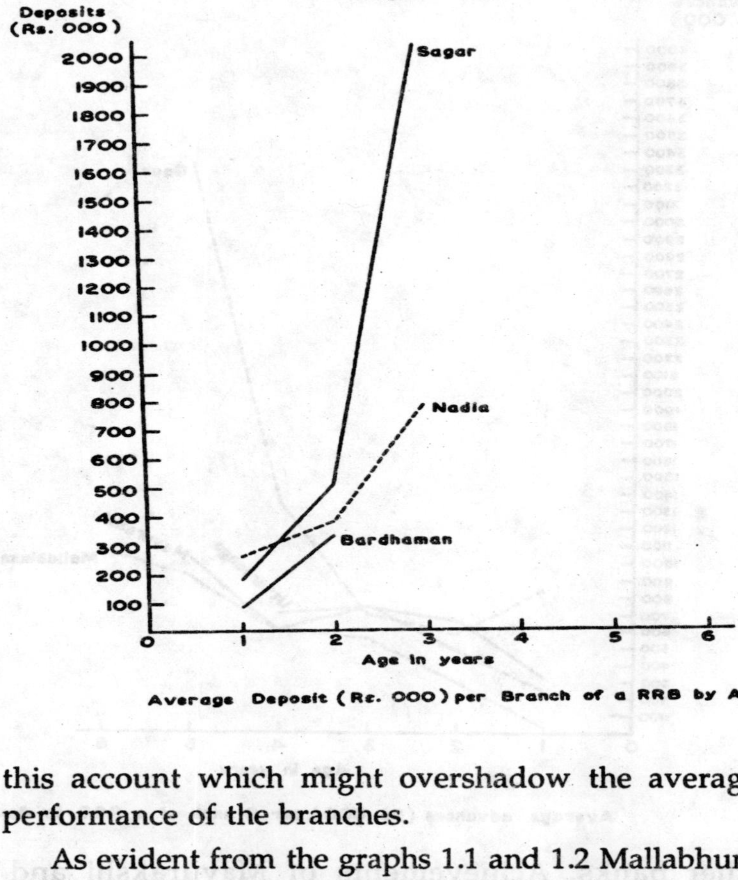

Average Deposit (Rs. 000) per Branch of a RRB by Age

this account which might overshadow the average performance of the branches.

As evident from the graphs 1.1 and 1.2 Mallabhum surpassed by far the other Regional Rural Banks in regard to the growth of deposits per branch. Progress of deposits per branch for Mayurakshi and Gaur was similar, but Uttarbanga experienced a sort of stagnation. Among the banks of recent origin Sagar proves to be highly progressive, Bardhaman lagging far behind. Nadia occupies a middle position on this score.

It may be seen from the figures 2.1 and 2.2 that advances per branch of Gaur sharply excel those of the

Figure 2·1

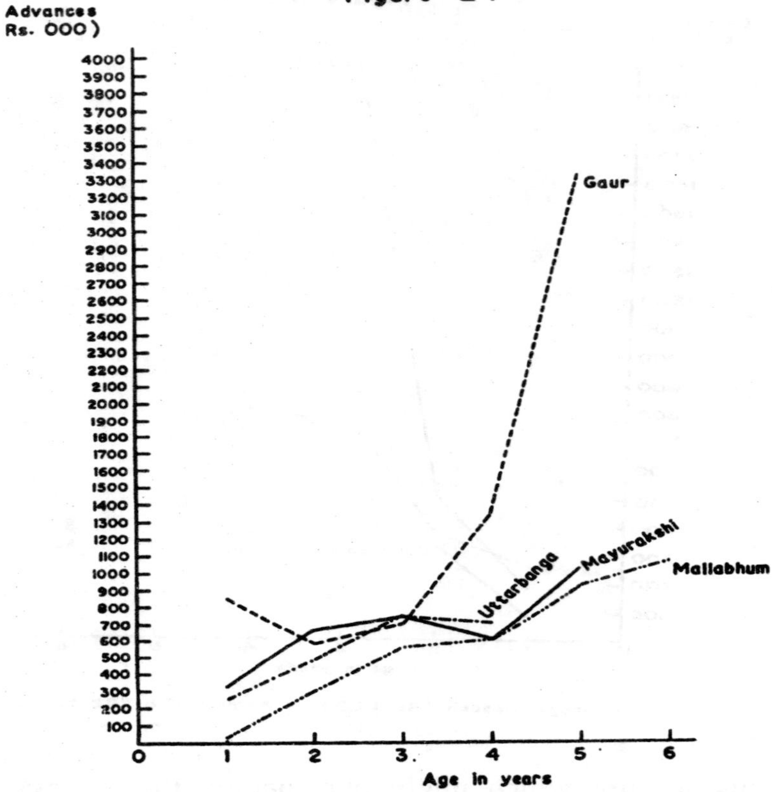

Average advances (Rs. 000) per Branch of a RRB by Age.

other banks. Achievements of Mayurakshi and Mallabhum on this score are almost similar, while Uttarbanga falls behind. Among new banks Sagar, again, scores a high progress of advances leaving Nadia and Bardhaman far behind.

Figure 3 is designed to show the extent of deposit mobilization and supply of credit per agricultural worker for each of the areas of operation of the Regional Rural Banks. Cultivators and agricultural labourers taken together are defined as agricultural workers who are

Figure 2·2

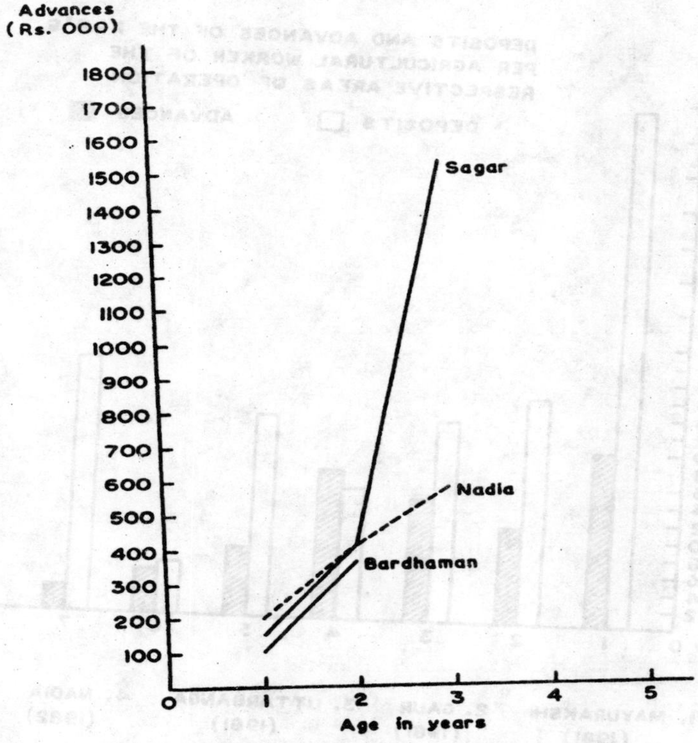

Average advances (Rs. 000) per Branch of a RRB by Age.

about 78% of the total rural labour-force. Therefore, the volume of credit and deposits can be properly assessed only in comparison with the total number of agricultural workers. In this respect, as is evident from Figure 3, with deposits of about Rs. 59/- and credit supply of Rs. 20/- per agricultural worker Mayurakshi occupies the most favourable position. The deposits of Gaur is Rs. 26/- and credit supply is Rs. 11/- per agricultural worker. The deposits of Uttarbanga is Rs. 23/- and credit supply is Rs. 14/- per agricultural worker. In case of

FIGURE - 3

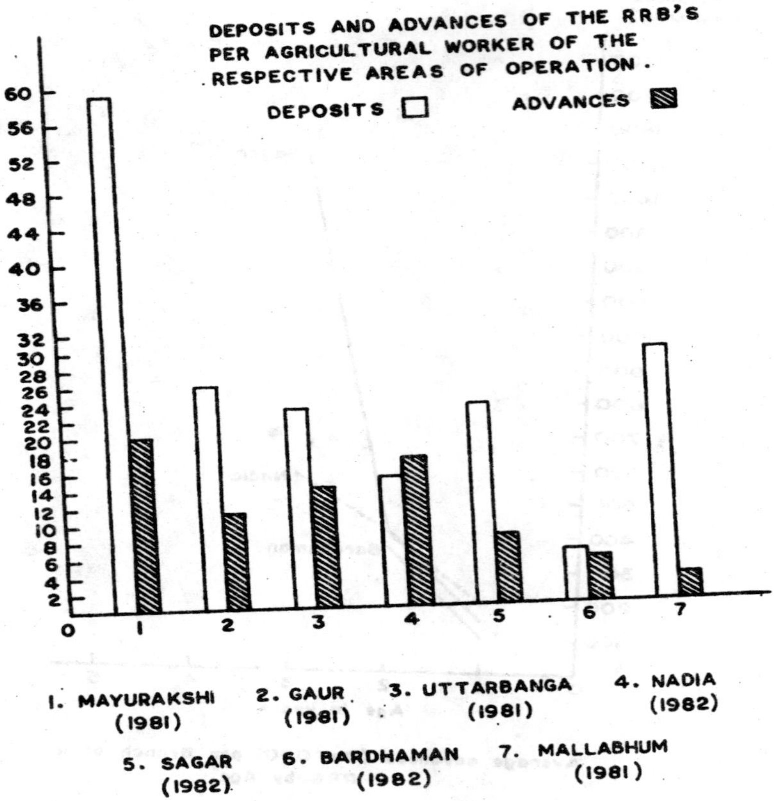

Mallabhum the deposits is Rs. 29/- and credit supply is Rs. 3/- per agricultural worker. The deposits of Nadia is Rs. 15/- and credit supply is Rs. 17/- per agricultural worker. The deposits of Sagar is Rs. 23/- and credit to the tune of Rs. 8/- per agricultural worker. The deposit and credit per agricultural worker of Bardhaman is Rs. 6/- and Rs. 5/- respectively.

In case of deposits the second position is captured by Mallabhum but credit supply is the lowest per agricultural worker. Among the new banks the deposits of Sagar is the highest per agricultural worker while the credit supply per agricultural worker is the highest in case of Nadia. However, in general it appears that the mobilization of deposits attained greater success than the supply of credit for agricultural worker.

The size of the area of operation of Mallabhum and its agricultural population seems to be too large to be handled by one Regional Rural Bank.

On the whole there is much more people of expansion on both the scores. This applies to all the Regional Rural Banks covered by this survey.

APPENDIX TO CHAPTER 7
COMMENTS ON THE KEEPING OF RECORDS BY REGIONAL RURAL BANKS

Since the case studies are based on material drawn mainly from the records of the Regional Rural Banks some comments on these records are felt necessary.

First of all, it appears that the Regional Rural Banks do not follow a uniform pattern of reporting. This is particularly for the classification of the types of loans. It is not enough to classify the loans as agricultural and non-agricultural or by broad activity-types. Specific Projects or activities of both agricultural and non-agricultural sectors to which credit is extended need to be defined. This is not done by most of the banks. Even if it is done in some cases there is little uniformity in categorization. Here the reports should be explicit about whether the loans are made for the acquisition of equipments and construction or for current production as working capital. This applies to both agricultural and non-agricultural sectors. In addition to sectoral classification, the loaning operations need to be classified at least under the following broad heads:

1. Fixed Capital Formation:
   - *(a)* Acquisition of equipments, period
   - *(b)* Construction, period
   - *(c)* Acquisition of animals.
2. Working Capital:
   - *(a)* Purchase of material inputs, period
   - *(b)* Marketing, period.
   - *(c)* Consumption of the borrower, period.

Records about recovery of loans furnished in Annual Reports of some of the banks are quite vague. These do not enable an investigator to form a definite idea of overdue loans. Records of recovery of loans need to be related to the age of debts.

Also, none of the reports specifies the sources of deposits, such as, private persons and public bodies or institutions. The record of sources will enable an investigator to form a clear picture of the pattern of mobilization of rural savings.

Bank records do not classify the borrowers according to their economic status, *e.g.*, size of holding, tenurial status (owner farmer or share-croppers) in the case of agricultural borrowers and assets in the case of the non-agricultural borrowers, *e.g.* artisans, shop-keepers, small-scale production etc. or according to the incomes of borrowers of both the sectors. Classification of the borrowers by economic status would enable an investigator to know fully the main characteristics of the recipients of loans.

Top of all, a uniform pattern of records-keeping and reporting should be formulated on the lines suggested above. This is absolutely necessary on the part of the banking authorities for properly monitoring and evaluating the performance of the Regional Rural Banks. Also, this will facilitate scientific credit-analysis and the formulation of appropriate future policies and programmes for the mobilization of rural savings and dispensation of rural credit.

8

Some Reflections on Structural and Operational Problems of Regional Rural Banks

Much of the success of a Regional Rural Bank will depend upon its structural soundness, adequacy of its resources, management and operational efficiency and the role of the associated agencies. This chapter is devoted to a discussion of requirements in all these respects which need to be satisfied or a Regional Rural Bank is expected to meet.

Requirements of Structural Efficiency

An important requirement of structural efficiency is determination of the area of operation of a RRB in an appropriate way. A RRB may fail to attain satisfactory progress if the area of its operation is not appropriate in terms of several criteria which may be laid down as follows:

Area of Operation and Branch Expansion

First of all, there should be scope for opening new branches and new branches can be opened in those places where banking facilities already available are quite meagre or insufficient and where population of the target groups is sizable. Compactness of geographical area, availability of infrastructural facilities, homogeneity of resources or types of production are also important factors that may influence decision in the matter.

The Chairmen of the RRBs at their conference held during 4-6 November, 1982 expressed their opinion that the area should be such as would provide scope for opening 80 branches and sufficient business. It, however, appears from the analysis of Chapter 7 that viability of a RRB would depend upon maintaining a volume of business that would conform to a low ratio between establishment and interest-cost. It would neither depend upon the number of branches nor on the extent of area of operation. Of course, compactness of area is desirable from the point of view of management.

As branch expansion was found to have been costly without being matched by proportionate return a caution needs to be sounded against rapid branch expansion without prior planning of appropriate personnel.

The area of operation should be such as will facilitate monitoring and supervision of branches. In the absence of arrangement for monitoring and adequate supervision by other than the head office, coverage of one district may be ideal for a RRB. A larger area, as in the case of

Mallabhum Gramin Bank, may result in neglect of supervision the impact of which on the efficiency of branch-operation would be adverse.

Share Capital

Since most of the RRBs were found to have been experiencing losses, there should be an assessment of real (exchangeable) value of their share capital after some years of their start. Measures may be taken for protection against fall in the exchangeable value of the share capital by fresh contributions from the concerned parties. It may also be considered whether NABARD can join other agencies in contributing share capital to the RRBs. It seems that subscribing additional share capital to cover the shortfall in the real/exchangeable value would be advantageous than the sharing of losses by the share-holders as the erosion could be recouped in later years on account of profitable working results.

Deposit Mobilization

As the deposits are the important resources of any bank and no less in the case of RRBs, mobilization of rural savings is an essential part to build up their resources. It appears that though the RRBs made good progress in the mobilization of rural savings, there is much scope of further progress when it is considered in relation to the total size of agricultural working population of the area of operation (Chapter 5). For giving impetus to such deposit mobilization in the long-run, the following measures may be kept in view:

1. As an incentive to the rural depositors, RRBs may be permitted to grant loans against deposits upto

a certain proportion of the face value of the deposits.

2. RRBs may be included in the approved list of banks of Central and State Governments for the purpose of keeping the surplus funds and operating the accounts of Government Departments, semi-Government bodies, Local bodies like Panchayats, Municipalities, Agricultural Product Market Committee etc.
3. The possibility of withdrawal of the restriction by the G.I.C. not to invest more than Rs. 50000 in a RRB may be considered.
4. Non-target groups, too, should be brought under the patronage of RRBs to a limited extent through some specific schemes of asset formation. This would stimulate rural development which in its turn would accentuate mobilization of rural savings.

Borrowings

RRBs are promoted mainly for meeting the credit requirements of weaker sections in the rural areas and so the refinance should fill the gap between mobilization of own resources and the total funding requirements of the rural poor. As the deposit mobilization potentiality is not uniform for all RRBs, the refinance terms should be flexible.

As deposit mobilization potentiality is not uniformly spread in the area of operation of all RRBs, the NABARD general line of refinance should be maintained.

RRBs must immediately form technical cells, either by re-deploying their existing officers who are otherwise qualified and suitable as mentioned earlier or by recruitment new staff for preparing schemes so that covering of term loans under schematic lending is stepped up. The necessary financial assistance for appointment of technical staff recently offered by NABARD may be utilised by the RRBs for the purpose.

Sponsor bank refinance is kept as a last resort by RRBs because of higher rate of interest at 81½%, while the refinance from other sources is cheaper. If it is desired to avail sponsor bank refinance on a larger scale, in preference to or on par with other refinance, it is necessary to consider whether the rate of interest charged by sponsor bank can be brought down from the present 81½% to that of NABARD's.

RRBs are experiencing administrative and procedural inconvenience/delays in availing of refinance from IDBI in respect of their small loans. So it is felt that a single agency approach *i.e.* obtaining refinance in respect of composite loans for artisans and rural industries etc. from NABARD would facilitate easy availability of refinance by RRBs.

Programme Development, Formulation of Scheme and Loan Policy

Absence of infrastructural facilities, conveyance facility, staff facilities, marketing facility are the constraints in the way of reaching the weaker section. This is reflected in low credit deposit-ratios of some of the RRB's (Chapter 5).

The RRBs should provide conveyance in the shape of cycles/moped/motor cycles to the Branch Managers/ Field staff so that they are more mobile and can reach remote places to contact the beneficiaries. Now RRBs may not be able to cope with the expenses on this head. Hence, sponsor banks should initially provide 3/4 motor cycles for the use of field work.

Pass books giving complete details of the beneficiaries about their land holdings, borrowings and other economic data should be invariably supplied and they should have a legal standing. It has been noted that RRBs or their branches do not keep detailed records of the economic status of the borrowers. These records are very necessary for the management of the loaning operations from sanction and disbursement to repayment (Appendix to Chapter 7).

The State Government should make wide publicity of the various schemes as RRBs are not in a position to spend much on this score. The State Government should also help in identification of the schemes which can be made applicable in a specified area. Expertise for formulation of schemes should also be made available by the State Government and sponsor banks.

It has been observed that staff of none of the Regional Rural Banks include technical personnel specialised in formulating projects to serve as guidelines for loaning operations (Chapter 5).

The RRBs should avail themselves of the facilities being extended by NABARD in the shape of financial help for the appointment of technical experts for creation of technical, monitoring and evaluation cell.

NABARD is making available automatic refinance for IRD loaning. This scheme should be extended to cover loaning under the DCP thereby making these loans eligible automatically for refinance. The schemes formulated therein are duly prepared by technical experts and approved by the State Government and implemented jointly with the banks in mutual consultation.

Specific schemes are required to be formulated keeping in view the socio-economic conditions prevalent in a particular area together with skills, resources and inputs etc. available there. As such there cannot be general schemes to be adopted by all the RRBs. However, on the basis of the area profile and indepth study of its economic condition, specific schemes should be formulated area-wise.

The proposal of technical cell, as already discussed, is a measure of great significance. The quantitative approach for coverage of the large number of borrowers may be indispensable, but the qualitative aspect should be constantly kept in sight. The project in those cases where incremental income is not sufficient enough to meet the entire needs of the target group, should be supplemented with innovative schemes to augment the income of the borrower to the extent that he has enough surplus with him to repay the loan after meeting basic necessities.

Extension work by the Government agencies should be linked with bank credit so that the productivity can be increased through adoption of modern techniques etc. wherever RRBs can afford they should be allowed to earmark some funds for the extension work also. Where it is found that either the loan or subsidy has been misutilised the Government should take firm action against the defaulters so that it may have some demonstrative effect on the other borrowers and such phenomena may be checked.

Consumption loan should also be linked with productive loans upto Rs. 1000/- wherever necessary so that some of the urgent needs of the poorer borrowers are not neglected. A package loan is therefore suggested to the identified family which is taken as a unit under IRDP.

RRBs should be allowed to encourage rural artisans, cottage/village and tiny industries. It is advisable that small artisans complex on the line of mini-industrial estates should be established by the State Government, and rented out to the beneficiaries. The RRBs should provide them financial assistance.

Within the prescribed limit of 40% of the total loans the RRBs should be allowed to continue to make advances against gold ornaments to target group for both agricultural and non-agricultural sectors. It is felt that if this is curtailed the poor borrower in search of money to meet his urgent requirements might be left to the mercy of the private money-lenders and thus defeat the very purpose of bringing him out of the clutches of the private money lenders. This also affects his repayment capacity.

Implementation of District Credit Plans and IRDP

Presently there are constraints in financing the beneficiaries on account of some of the schemes which are unbankable, tight resources position of the RRBs and absence of the forward and backward linkage effect of the project.

Difficulties experienced by the RRBs for providing assistance to the IRDP beneficiaries and the implementation of the 20-Point Economic Programme are as follows:

(*a*) Identification of the borrowers is not proper which leads to duplicity of efforts.

(*b*) The agencies lay more stress on quantitative aspect of lending to achieve their targets and in the process the qualitative aspect is neglected. This requires to be rectified.

(*c*) Proper guidance is not given to the borrowers by the sponsoring agencies about the schemes offered to them.

The RRBs are facing constraints on account of the following factors as well:

(*a*) The schemes formulated are often not bankable as the DRDA do not have good experience to formulate the schemes.

(*b*) There is more stress on achieving the target and in the absence of monitoring it is not known to what extent the borrowers have been benefitted by the schemes. The constant monitoring process is thus a necessity.

(*c*) To make co-ordination more effective Government functionaries DCC meetings should give m more weightage to the point of views expressed by the banks in the Committee. It would be more appropriate if the bankers are associated in the formulation of Annual Plan by DRDA, DICs and other developmental agencies.

State Government's Assistance

(*a*) It is felt that for having a branch of Regional Rural Bank at a particular centre, the minimum infrastructural facilities should be made available by the State Government, including

(*i*) Pacca house, for branch premises along with

residence of the Branch Manager as is being done by Haryana Government.

(ii) Means of transport and communication.

(iii) Post Office.

(iv) Police Stations in the nearby areas.

(b) (i) The State Government should issue pass-books showing details of land held by the farmers, as recommended by Baldev Singh Committee.

(ii) Identification of the beneficiaries under District Rural Development Agency and other Government Schemes should be done by the concerned government agencies.

(iii) Subsidy should be released in advance to the bank as prescribed so that disbursement is faster.

(iv) All developmental activities of the Regional Rural Banks should be invariably reviewed at the meeting of the State Level Bank Committee, State Level Coordination Committee for Regional Rural Banks, and problems coming in the way of their functioning should be solved in State Level Coordination Committee of which all Regional Rural Banks should be members.

(c) Recoveries: Case studies have already revealed that recoveries of loans of the Regional Rural Banks were not satisfactory (Chapter 5).

(i) A special cell should be formed by the State Government with the involvement of the local Panchayat, Government agencies like District Rural Development Agency towards recovery of loans made under District Rural Development Agency/ other Government schemes by various agencies.

(ii) Talwar Committee recommendations for amendment of laws of recovery of Government

revenues like Public Demand Recovery (PDR) Act should be implemented. Bank loans may be recovered as Government dues under Public Recovery Act as in force in U.P. for agricultural loans and non-agricultural loans.

(iii) Non-agricultural loans are also to be governed by the same rules.

9

Summary and Conclusions

Important developments taking place in the Indian Banking System during the last three decades led to the widening of the role of the institutional credit agencies. Attempt was made to revitalise the cooperative movement by state-participation, production-oriented credit policy and reorganisation of weak societies into viable ones. The year 1969 witnessed the nationalisation of 14 major commercial banks followed by 6 more in 1980. As a result, there was considerable branch expansion of commercial banks even in rural areas.

Cooperatives lacked managerial competence and were subservient to the interests of predominant social groups. The commercial banks, on the other hand, were handicapped by high cost of establishment caused by new branches. Their urban orientation and inadequate understanding of the rural problems prevented them from meeting the needs of the rural poor. Hence the gap between the demand for and supply of rural credit was not narrowed significantly. Rather, it increased considerably owing to the introduction of the High Yielding Variety technology in agriculture which greatly added to the financial requirements of farming. Private money-lenders still continued to be predominant. Institutional credit on fair terms and conditions was still beyond the reach of the weaker sections of the community. Particularly in West Bengal the lower asset position of the average cultivator and the weaker condition of the rural economy in general in comparison with that in other states accentuated the need of institutional credit for the rural poor.

Inadequacy of the traditional banking system gave rise to the need of a specialised institution like Regional Rural Banks combining resource and competence of the commercial banks with the rural orientation and democratic approach of the cooperatives as well as low cost of establishment. The year 1975 marked the establishment of five Regional Rural Banks in India for the first time following the recommendations of the Working Group on Rural Banks with M. Narasimham as its Chairman.

Case-studies of seven Regional Rural Banks except the Howrah Gramin Bank were undertaken with a view to collecting detailed data on their structure and functioning. The study involved intensive field investigation into the conditions of Regional Rural Banks of West Bengal. As the Howrah Gramin Bank was a new entrant in the field of rural banking when the study was being conducted, no data were available from it.

A comparative assessment of the seven Regional Rural Banks is given to show the performance of these banks in various respects. It is seen that some of them earned profit while majority suffered from losses in successive years. Causes of losses have been identified by analysis of costs of RRBs (Chapter 7) to be an imbalance between establishment cost and the volume of investments or loaning business. The total volume of business in the cases of Regional Rural Banks suffering losses was found to be not in conformity with the establishment cost. It is the volume of business undertaken by a RRB which matters most. Poor recovery of loans might have been one of the factors which adversely affected the volume of loaning business by hindering recycling of loanable funds. It is, therefore, all the more desirable that the volume of business should be large enough to compensate the losses due to poor recovery. Multiplication of branches added to total cost more than in proportion to the total volume of investment.

It appears from the case studies that the objective of setting up institutions specialized in extending credit to weaker sections of the rural community has been substantially fulfilled by the Regional Rural Banks. It is evident from the fact that the branches of the RRB have achieved tangible progress in supplying credit to the rural poor and bringing some of the remotest parts of rural area of West Bengal within the fold of organised banking system. Crop loans advanced by the RRBs are particularly meant for share-croppers, marginal and small farmers. Since these loans are available at moderate rates of interest not exceeding 12.50% without much stringency about collateral they meet some real need of the weaker sections of the community in the realm of credit (Chapter 6).

The quantum of credit is fixed in such a way as to cover the entire cost of cultivation (Chapter 6). This adds to their benefit.

However, there is further need for liberalizing the provision for consumption credit for which the rural borrowers are still under pressure to depend on private money lenders.

An objective of RRBs was to supply rural credit at lower administrative cost with greater degree of rural orientation in comparison with the commercial banks and at greater level of efficiency than that of the cooperative banks. The degree of fulfilment of this objective is still not beyond question, since volume of loaning operations of the RRBs has been revealed by case studies not commensurate with the cost of establishment (Chapter 7).

The case studies indicate that the RRBs have experienced high rate of growth of deposits on their savings bank accounts. However, there still seems to be further scope of mobilization of savings with regard to the agricultural working population of the area of operation of a RRB (Chapter 7).

The loanable funds of the RRBs should be more liberally augmented by borrowings from the Reserve Bank of India, sponsoring banks, NABARD and other agencies to stimulate growth of savings bank deposits of the RRBs as well as their loaning operations.

There is great scope of improving business efficiency of the Regional Rural Banks by addition of a technical cell to the existing staff of the banks. The technical cell should be preoccupied with the formulation of location-specific investment projects based on appropriate field studies. This would go a lonkg way toward enabling the Regional Rural Banks to enhance the rate of profitable utilisation of credit and raise the credit-deposit ratio which was found to be low in the case of many of the Regional Rural Banks.

Since poor recovery of loans is a common problem for most of the RRBs, adequate arrangement for the monitoring and supervision of the activities of the recipients of credit should be made. Also legislative measures applicable to the recovery of public dues should be extended to the case of loans made by the RRBs.

Area of operation in the cases of some of the Regional Rural Banks has been found to be too extensive to make it possible for them to bring their service to the doors of most of the potential customers. Thus this was found to have hindered both the mobilisation of rural savings and extension of credit. There should be at least one Regional Rural Bank for each of the administrative districts.

The keeping of records of the RRBs should be more elaborate and uniform so that inter-comparison is made possible for evaluation and the formulation of common improvement policies.

Bibliography

Agro-Economic Research Centre, Visva-Bharati, Agricultural Development in West Bengal - Mimeograph 1977, Vol. I & II.

Agricultural Census 1976-77, Board of Revenue, Directorate of Agriculture, Government of West Bengal, 1979, p. 10.

All India Rural Credit Survey, Vol. II, p. 218.

Bardhaman Gramin Bank, Annual Reports, 1980, 1981 and 1982.

Census of India, 1971.

Census of India, 1981.

Das Gupta D.K., *Regional Imbalances in Agricultural Growth in West Bengal.*

Das Amal Kumar, *The West Bengal Land Reforms Act, 1955 and Rules,* Published by R.K. Sahu, 104/4/4, Satyen Roy Road, Calcutta-34.

Datta, Bhabatosh, *The Contents of Economic Growth and other Essays.*

Datta, Bhabatosh, Regional Rural Banks, *Economic and Political Weekly*, Bombay, Vol. XIII, No. 36, September 9, 1978.

Directorate of Cottage and Small Scale Industries, Government of West Bengal.

Gaur Gramin Bank, *Annual Reports, 1975, 1976, 1977, 1978, 1979, 1980 and 1981.*

Government of India, Report of the Agricultural Finance Sub-Committee, New Delhi, 1945, p. 59.

Government of India, The Indian Central Banking Enquiry Committee Majority Report, New Delhi, 1931, p. 77.

Government of India, Department of Revenue and Banking, Report of the Expert Committee on Consumption Credit (Chairman, B. Sivaraman), New Delhi, April 1976, Chapter 5.

Government of India, *Report of the Committee (Working Group) on Rural Banks*, New Delhi, 1975.

Government of India, *Report of the National Commission on Agriculture*, New Delhi, 1976, Part XII, Para 55.7.11.

Government of West Bengal Bureau of Applied Economics and Statistics—Statistical Handbook, 1979.

Government of West Bengal, *Economic Review, 1980-81*.

Gaikwad, V.R., 'Participation of Rural Institutions and Target Groups in Rural Development Programme Planning and Management, Working Paper No. 217, Ahmedabad, Indian Institute of Management, June 1978, and Ghiara, B.M., "Agricultural Financing by Commercial Banks: A Look Ahead", *Prajnan*, Vol. VI, No. 3, July-September, 1977, p. 286.

Government of West Bengal, Land Reforms in West Bengal, 1979.

Government of West Bengal, An Evaluation of a Pledge, 1980.

Government of West Bengal, Left Front Government and Some Aspects of Its Activities in Rural Areas, 1980.

Government of India, *Report of the Banking Commission,* 1972.

Joshi, P.N., "Regional Rural Banks", *The Journal of the Indian Institute of Bankers,* Vol. 47, No. 2, April-June, 1976.

Mayurakshi Gramin Bank, *Annual Reports, 1976, 1977, 1978, 1979, 1980 and 1981.*

Mallabhum Gramin Bank, *Annual Reports 1976, 1977, 1978, 1979, 1980 and 1981.*

Madhu S. Misra, Need for Appraisal and a New Strategy in Rural Development—Action and Management, Indian Institute of Management, Calcutta, 1981.

Mandal, G.C., Ghosh, M.G., *Economics of Green Revolution,* Asia Publishing House, Bombay, 1976, pp. 63-66.

Nadia Gramin Bank, *Annual Reports, 1980, 1981, 1982.*

Reserve Bank of India, 1970, History of the RBI (1935-51).

Registration of Cooperative Societies, West Bengal.

RBI, *All India Rural Credit Survey,* Vol. II, Chapter 8 and 9.

RBI, *Report on Currency and Finance,* Vol. I, 1976-77, pp. 131.2.

RBI, *Statistical Statements Relating to the Cooperative Movement in India, 1975-76,* Part I, Bombay, Credit Societies, 1977.

Report of the Expert Committee on Consumption Credit, Chapter 2.

Report of the All-India Rural Credit Review Committee, Report of the Committee on Rural Banks. Reserve Bank of India, Report of the Study team on Overdues of Cooperative Credit Institutions, Bombay, 1974 and RBI, Report of the Committee on Integration of Cooperative Credit Institutions, Bombay, 1976.

Report of the Committee on Integration of Cooperative Credit Institutions, pp. 26-7.

Report of the Conference of RRBs held in New Delhi from 4th to 6th November, 1982.

Report of the Committee on Rural Banks, New Delhi 1975.

Sagar Gramin Bank, *Annual Reports, 1980, 1981 and 1982.*

Sengupta, S. and P.D. Joshi, "A Note on the Determination of Poverty line based on National Sample Survey 27th Round data, *Sarvekshan,* Vol. III, No. 1, July 1979.

Statistical Statements Relating to the Cooperative Movement in India 1975-76.

Statistical Statements Relating to the Cooperative Movement in India 1975-76, Part I.

The Economic Times, Calcutta, Saturday, June 26, 1982.

Uttarbanga Kshetriya Gramin Bank, Annual Reports, 1977, 1978, 1979, 1980 and 1981.

Various issues of the *RBI Bulletin.*

Wadhva, D. Charan, *Rural Banks for Rural Development,* The Macmillan Company of India Limited, 1980.

